THE MESSIAH REVEALED

A BIBLE STUDY OF THE LETTER TO THE HEBREWS

CARA SMITH

Dedication

This study was originally written for the Bible study groups at The Chapel in Akron, Ohio in 2015. This version is dedicated to the women who studied the Word of God so diligently in those original groups.

TO:

Michael for his tireless support for my work and his secret Tuesday morning work in the children's program.

Daniel, Claire, Will, Mark, Ingrid and Ivy with love and hope that you will trust always in the revealed Messiah, Jesus.

Sallie Stalnaker for her example of joyful, diligent study and her soft-hearted obedience to what she hears in the Word of God. For being one of my first encouragers in my role as leader of leaders.

Table of Contents

Welcome

Thanks for choosing *The Messiah Revealed: A Bible study of the Letter to the Hebrews.* This study is written for a small group Bible study that values both in-depth personal study and lively group discussion. I am convinced that any believer can understand and apply the Bible to his or her own life through thorough personal preparation and group discussion.

Because the Bible is God's Word, it has the ability to speak to you in ways that other books do not. In 2 Timothy 3:16-17 it teaches that Scripture is "breathed out by God and profitable for teaching, for reproof, for correction and for training in righteousness, that the man of God may be competent, equipped for every good work." (ESV) Therefore, your personal interaction with Scripture is an interaction with God himself. By engaging with God, employing sound Bible study techniques and developing consistent study habits you can become a confident, competent Bible student. This kind of hands-on Bible study helps you not only master the text, but also lets the God who "breathed out" the text master you. It leads you to obedience, true life-change and equips you for good work.

Once you have studied and interacted with the Scriptures for yourself, group discussion provides further insight and perspective. When each member has invested time in personal study the discussion is informed and rich. But small group interaction is about more than learning. When a group of believers meet with the Word of God as their focus, something else happens. They humbly engage with one another, provide encouragement, accountability and the love it takes to live Christ-like, Spirit-directed, Bible-informed lives. They experience truth and love.

Study Method

This study is written from a guided inductive approach. The questions are open-ended and will require you to think for yourself. The study will occasionally provide limited commentary, but the purpose of this method is to guide discovery, not to provide teaching and answers. The inductive method includes observation, interpretation and application questions.

Each numbered question of the study will have at least one type of question. Often, you will find that a numbered question has several layered questions. These are meant to guide your thought process and often include more than one type of question. Understanding the types of questions will help you enter into the inductive process and produce appropriate answers to the questions. To understand how to recognize observation, interpretation and application questions keep reading!

Observation

Observation questions answer: *What does the text say?* Good observation leads you to look at the text objectively and factually. You'll know an observation question because it asks for a direct answer from the text. These questions bring out the "who, what, when, where, why and how" of the passage. Sometimes there will be charts to fill out or lists to make that help you observe and organize the text. Try to keep from interpreting or applying as you answer these questions. Don't avoid these questions because they seem obvious or dismiss them as easy. Observation questions set the groundwork for later interpretation and application. After all, how can we decide what a passage means or how we should apply it to our lives if we haven't first closely observed was it actually says? (See more about this process in the *Observation* page in the Appendix.)

Interpretation

Interpretation questions answer: *What does the text mean?* Cross-referencing, word studies, and examining context are all tools for understanding what the passage means to its fullest. Many of the questions will ask you to paraphrase or summarize what the text is saying. When you do this, you are interpreting. Some will ask directly what the passage means. This is a cue to use your cross-references and look up words even if the question doesn't provide them. (See more in the *Cross-reference* and *Word Study* pages in the Appendix.)

Application

Application questions answer: *What should I do?* Application questions are open-ended and could have many different answers. They are meant to be probing and personal. Sometimes they will be encouraging; at other times they will be convicting or challenging. Always, they are meant to spur you to action! All three types of questions are important, but application is the ultimate goal of Bible study. We must be doers of the Word, not merely hearers (James 1:22.) Don't skip these questions! Pray, ponder and open yourself up to the work of God as you think through the application questions.

Sometimes you will discover your own applications or ask you own questions. This is great and a vital part of the inductive process. Ask and answer your own questions!

Resource Guidelines

This study is written using the *English Standard Version* (ESV) of the Bible. You will need a good translation of the Bible with faithfulness to the original Greek and Hebrew texts. ESV, NASB or NIV translations with cross-references will work for this study. "Living" translations or paraphrases like *The Message* are valuable for devotional reading but are not best for this type of inductive study.

You will occasionally need an English dictionary or a Greek expository dictionary such as *The Complete Word Study Dictionary – New Testament* by Spiros Zodhiates. Bible websites such as blueletterbible.org also provide resources for word study. (See *Word Study* in the *Study Aids* Appendix for more information.)

You will not need commentaries for this study. Feel free to consult commentaries and the study notes in your Bible *after* you have done your homework. Scholarship is good and is to be utilized only after you have done your own work at understanding a passage. It is just too easy to shortcut study by going immediately to commentaries. It prevents your development as a student and deprives you of the thrill of personal discovery you get when you have worked through a passage for yourself. A small amount of commentary is provided in each lesson.

Be warned! A dynamic can develop within a group that shuts down discussion when a member consistently quotes their favorite commentator. If you do consult commentaries, consult more than one trusted commentator, and be aware that you will very likely get more than one opinion! Your own study will help you discern the relative value of those opinions. There are some trusted commentaries listed in the bibliography.

How to Use This Study

Complete one lesson per week. It will take *at least* two hours of personal study to complete a lesson. The lesson has section titles built into it to indicate a change of topic. Some people may want to use these sections as a daily study segment. Others may prefer to do their personal study in one longer session.

It will take a group two hours to discuss a lesson and have some time to pray for one another. The most logical flow for discussion is to do the questions in numerical order. You may want to move more quickly through the observation questions, since they are typically more objective. This leaves plenty of time for discussion when interpretation and application questions come. Don't feel compelled to discuss every question. Sometimes a group will profit by focusing on a certain aspect of the study, depending on the needs of the group, so flexibility can be good. That being said, avoid going too far off topic. Rabbit trails are usually counter-productive and frustrating for most members of the group.

At my home church leaders prepare together in a weekly leader's training group. We discuss the lesson and get input from one another and also have training on the various skills necessary to lead a group well. This extra layer of support is valuable for leaders but is not necessary. With diligent preparation, any mature believer with good interpersonal skills and a will to facilitate discussion could lead this material. Under this mature leadership, even a believer with no Bible study experience can grow using this material.

Life Story Day

You'll notice in the Appendix of this study there is a section called *Life Story Days*. I encourage your group to schedule four meetings when you concentrate on sharing your life stories. This kind of sharing builds group bonds and provides an atmosphere of true fellowship. I have seen over and over in both men's and women's groups that *Life Story Days* inspire relational openness and authentic life sharing that wouldn't otherwise happen. I strongly encourage you to spread these *Life Story Days* throughout your year together. For a more thorough description of *Life Story Days* and the question prompts that go with them, see the Appendix.

OVERVIEW

In our first lesson we will acquaint ourselves with the book as a whole. We will look at its structure, the main topics it covers, the repeated themes and the exhortations it addresses to the Hebrew people for whom it was originally written. This lesson gives us good groundwork and sets us up to understand the message of the book as a whole.

As you work through the overview it is important to have an inquisitive outlook that generates questions. You won't be *answering* all of your questions, but take courage! You are preparing to receive the truth this book has to offer in the coming weeks.

Who, What, Where, When, Why and How

1. Read the whole book of Hebrews in one sitting. (This will take you at least 30 minutes.) As you read I want you to look for answers to the following "who, what, where, why, when, and how" questions and jot down verses that you think help answer: (These are preliminary thoughts just to help you read with purpose. Don't get bogged down, and don't worry about getting everything.)

Who wrote and received this book? (There aren't obvious answers, so look for clues and descriptions)

What concepts or topics are repeated?

What situations or problems might the readers be facing?

Where are the readers?

When is this letter written? (Try to guess whether or not the destruction of the Temple that happened in 70 A.D. has happened yet.)

Why is the author writing this letter?

What emotions seem to be behind the writing of this letter?

Let's Make an Outline

2. Constructing an outline will also help us begin to get the overall picture of the book. There are many ways to outline. You will find one possible example below. Read each section quickly and provide a *brief* title for it. If you were doing a full outline you could also do sub-points for each section. For now, just write a title for each section that includes the main point or topic for that section.

I.   The Superiority of Faith in Jesus

Hebrews 1:1-4

Hebrews 1:5-2:18

Hebrews 3:1-19

Hebrews 4:1-13

Hebrews 4:14-5:10

Hebrews 5:11-6:12

Hebrews 6:13-20

Hebrews 7:1-28

Hebrews 8:1-13

Hebrews 9:1-10

Hebrews 9:11-28

Hebrews 10:1- 18

II.   The Practice of Faith in Jesus

Hebrews 10:19-39

Hebrews 11:1-40

Hebrews 12:1-17

Hebrews 12:18-29

Hebrews 13:1-6

Hebrews 13:7-25

Better

3. Scan the titles that you wrote for each section. You probably have noticed that one of the main ways the author makes his points is to compare the lesser to the greater. We see the words "better," "superior," and "more excellent" repeated. Not all of these passages contain these words, but they do have comparisons or contrasts. For each passage note who or what is better and who or what it is better than.

Example:
Hebrews 1:4
Jesus is superior to angels, and he has a more excellent name than angels.

Hebrews 3:3-6

Hebrews 3:18-19; 4:8-10

Hebrews 7:11,18-19

Hebrews 7:22

Hebrews 7:23-28

Hebrews 8:6-7

Hebrews 9:11-14

Hebrews 9:23-24

Hebrews 9:25-26

Hebrews 10:11-12

Hebrews 10:39-40

Hebrews 12:3-4

Hebrews 12:9-10

Hebrews 12:20-24

Hebrews 12:25

4. How do these comparisons show the author's purpose in writing the letter? How are these specific comparisons tailored for his audience?

Exhortations

5. Hebrews is a letter filled with deep theology, but it is also very practical and contains many exhortations. These exhortations often come after the word "therefore" in the text. To get a preview of all the great encouragement and exhortation we will study this year look up the following "therefore," "for," and "but" transitions and note what action or hope is encouraged.

Hebrews 2:1

Hebrews 3:1

Hebrews 3:12-14

Hebrews 4:1

Hebrews 4:11

Hebrews 6:1

Hebrews 6:11-12

Hebrews 10:19-25

Hebrews 11:35-38

Hebrews 12:1-2

Hebrews 12:12-16

Hebrews 12:28

Hebrews 13:13-16

6. There are many action points here! Rather than trying to make application for our lives at this point, let's think of at least 5 problems the Hebrew people may have had that these exhortations address.

7. How do these exhortations give us more insight into the author's purpose for his letter?

Summarize

8. OK, you have already studied really hard! Our purpose in this first study was to get acquainted with the letter so that as we look at it little by little over the coming lessons, we will understand each passage's context within the whole. Go back to the first question and add in any new insights you got from the rest of the study. Then read the introduction to the book of Hebrews in a study Bible (or two). Add in any other insight on the "who, what, where, why, when and how" questions.

9. For your final exercise try to write a summary of the book of Hebrews in three sentences or fewer!

THE SUPERIORITY OF THE SON

Hebrews 1:1-3

The author of Hebrews boldly asserts that "God spoke" in his opening line.

God exists, and he wants to be known, so he spoke the world and humanity into existence. Then he began to progressively reveal himself to mankind. First in many times and in many ways through the prophets but eventually he became incarnate in the Son. In these last days he spoke through Jesus. Let's listen!

God Speaks

1. The writer of The Letter to The Hebrews starts his letter in a unique way. Read Hebrews 1:1-3, and then check the beginning of several other epistles. How is the opening of this letter different from the others? What is missing?

2. Some commentators suggest that this is more of a sermon than a typical letter. If so, he starts the sermon off very strongly! He affirms the life-changing truth that "God spoke." What does Hebrews 1:1 say about how God spoke?

3. Look up the following passages to get a sampling of these many ways:

Genesis 46:1-3

Exodus 6:2-9

Leviticus 1:1-2

Numbers 9:15-23

Deuteronomy 4:12-15

2 Samuel 7:7-17

Jeremiah 36:1-4

4. In Hebrews 1:1 it says that God spoke through the prophets. When God spoke through prophets, what should have been people's proper response? How does this match with what Scriptures say the actual response often was? Read Matthew 23:29-37; Luke 16:29-31 and Acts 7:52.

5. Why do you think mankind responds in this way? (Use Scripture if you can.)

6. Hebrews 1:2 reveals a new way God has spoken. How has God spoken in these last days? What do you think this means?

7. Use Matthew 5:17-18 and 2 Peter 1:16-21 to connect the Son to prophecy. What are the origins of prophecy and to whom does prophecy point? What do these passages say to do because of this?

8. List the qualifications that make his Son different than the prophets from Hebrews 1:2-3.

Son of God

9. The first descriptor is that Jesus is the Son of God. Look up these passages to get an idea what this means.

Matthew 3:17

Matthew 9:6

Matthew 11:27

Matthew 12:8

Matthew 16:16

Matthew 17:5

John 6:27

John 8:28

John 20:21

10. What conclusions do you draw about the relationship between the Father and the Son?

Heir

11. The next description of Jesus is that he is the "heir of all things." Use these passages to write a summary of what this means:

Matthew 28:18

John 3:35

John 10:29

John 16:15

John 17:2-6

Summary:

Creator

12. In Hebrews 2:2 it also says that God created the world through Jesus. Look up John 1:1-3 to confirm this. Why does it matter that Jesus is creator? Try to think of at least three reasons.

13. Compare Colossians 1:15-20 to Hebrews 1:2-3. Make a list of all you learn about Jesus.

Colossians   **Hebrews**

His Worth and Work

14. There are three interesting words in the description found in Hebrews 1:3. Use an expository Bible dictionary to look up "radiance," "exact imprint," and "upholds" in the Greek. What insights do you gain into Jesus identity? (You may also want to cross-reference.)

Radiance:

Exact Imprint:

Upholds:

15. In the end of Hebrews 1:3 it says that Jesus sat down at the right hand of God. This indicates that he took a place of honor after he had finished his work. What was this work, and what do the previous verses say about his qualifications to accomplish this work?

The Real Jesus

16. If Jesus really is who Hebrews 1:2-3 says he is then it is of utmost importance that we study and come to know the biblical (real) Jesus. What misconceptions of Jesus' person and his work do you hear commonly in our culture?

17. Surveys have shown that when Christians are asked to list their own character qualities and the character qualities of Jesus, the strongest pattern that emerges is that most people think Jesus has the same positive qualities that they themselves possess. In other words, most people fashion Jesus in their own image. What is the danger here? What are two practical ways you can combat this tendency?

18. How could the *truth* about Jesus from Hebrews 1:1-3 inspire trust and perseverance during trial or temptation for the original readers of the book of Hebrews?

19. Why are these truths about Jesus always a good starting point when our faith is tested or sags? Why are they better than concentrating on the trial?

20. Let's go back to the beginning of our lesson. If God has spoken, and he has spoken through his Son, who is supremely qualified, what should our response be to what he says? (For some ideas read Matthew 17:5; John 14:23 and 15:4, 9-12.)

21. When you think of obedience, what comes to mind? Is there an area of disobedience in your life that God is asking you to take seriously? What would be first steps toward listening to and abiding in Christ in that area?

TURN THE PAGE FOR THE END OF THE LESSON

Go back over this lesson and make a list of truth you found about Jesus' character and work. We will use this list throughout the year to help us create a clear, accurate picture of our savior, and to worship him rightly.

<u>JESUS</u>

BETTER THAN ANGELS

Hebrews 1:4-2:18

After his rich description of Jesus in the opening of the letter to the Hebrews, the author begins to elaborate on his thesis that Jesus is superior to all of the ways Jews had worshiped in the past. His first contrast is odd to modern ears. He says Jesus is superior to angels. Though angels have made their way into popular culture, they certainly are not the angelic beings described in the Bible. In this lesson we will learn about angels and also follow the argument that Jesus is worthy of worship because he is better than angels in both his deity and humanity!

Angels

1. We are going to start this lesson in a little different way. In order to process the writer's argument clearly, we need to have a biblical view of angels. So, we are not going to start in our passage. We are going to start with cross-references. Fill in the chart below listing the attributes and actions of angels and reactions that people had when they encountered angels. (Not all references will have information for both categories.)

	Attribute/Action	People's Reactions
Psalm 91:11-12		
Matthew 1:20-24		
Matthew 4:10-11		
Matthew 13:39-49		
Matthew 26:53		
Matthew 28:2-9		
Luke 1:11-25		
Luke 1:26-39		
Luke 2:9-16		

Luke 15:10

Acts 5:19-21

Acts 7:30-38

Revelation 5:11-14

2. In Lesson two we noticed that when God spoke through the prophets and even when he spoke through the Son many times there was contempt or disobedience. Draw some conclusions (from the above references) about the reactions of people when they encounter angels.

3. Why do you think angels inspired such a different reaction? How might this have confused people about who was worthy of worship and so brought up the first topic of this letter? (Check also Colossians 2:18.)

4. Our culture is also confused about angels. What are some of the common views of angels? Why do you think people are attracted to these portrayals? How might these portrayals lead people away from Christ and biblical truth?

5. Ok, now let's dig into our passage. Read Hebrews 1:4-2:18. Notice that the author uses many quotations as the author argues his points. From where does the author quote in Hebrews 1:5-13; 2:6-8, 12-13? Why do you think this approach was taken for these readers?

Better than Angels

6. The sentence begun in Hebrews 1:3 is ended in Hebrews 1:4. After giving the description of the Son in Hebrews 1:1-3, what conclusion does he draw in 1:4?

7. Look up the word "angel" in a Greek expository dictionary of the New Testament, and also in the Hebrew. What is the meaning of "angel"?

8. To explain what else he means by a "superior name," the author continues the theme that God has spoken. Find and note all the verses in Hebrews 1:5-14 where you see the verbs, "say," "says," and "said." Why does he emphasize that *God* has spoken when quoting Old Testament Scripture? Why would this matter to Jewish readers?

9. Fill in the chart below to gather the information that shows the contrast between the Son and angels. If there are phrases or descriptions you don't understand underline them.

The Son	Angels
1:5	
1:6	
1:7	

The Son	Angels
1:8-9	
1:10-12	
1:13	
1:14	

10. Use cross-references or word studies to clarify at least one of your underlined statements from question 9. What did you find out?

11. The author has made a bold case that Jesus is God and worthy of worship and that angels are subservient to him. They are ministers to those who are saved. Take some time to worship God in Christ for these superior attributes. Write out your worship here.

Don't Drift

12. Notice the transition word "therefore" in Hebrews 2:1. He is about to draw an application that goes with all that he has taught about angels and Jesus. Read Hebrews 2:1-4. What is the author's admonition in 2:1?

13. The argument in Hebrews 2:1-4 is from the lesser to the greater. If the messages of angels are reliable, then how much more the declarations of God! What message was declared by God and what three evidences does Hebrews 2:3-4 give to verify it?

14. We are warned against drifting from or neglecting this great salvation. How do you think the modern church has both drifted from and neglected the true gospel message? (Think of some very popular false gospels.)

15. How might you in particular be tempted to drift from the gospel? How can you keep yourself from such danger? Use cross-references and think of at least three ways!

Lower than Angels

16. Chapter 2 takes an interesting turn now. Up until this point Jesus' superiority and deity have been emphasized, especially compared to angels. Now his incarnation as a man is emphasized for the ways it is superior to the angels. Use Hebrews 2:5-14 to explain the ideas that Jesus is both higher and lower than the angels:

Higher than Angels   **Lower than Angels**

17. In Hebrews 2:10-11 it gives us the great assurance that Jesus' suffering as a man accomplishes great things for us. What does it accomplish?

18. As you are in the process of growing as a believer, how does it help to think that Jesus is not ashamed to call you brother (or sister)? How does that change the way you view Jesus and yourself?

19. Because of Jesus' humanity he is uniquely positioned to save and help mankind. Read Hebrews 2:14-18. For each verse write what Jesus has accomplished for mankind:

2:14

2:15

2:16

2:17

2:18

Jesus Helps

20. Hebrews 2:14-18 describes a victory already won and also the sweet promise of hope amid the current struggles of fear and temptation. What fears and temptations are you currently facing? What is behind these fears and temptations for you?

21. Review these Scripture passages on temptation:

Matthew 6:13

Matthew 26:41

1 Corinthians 10:12-13

James 1:12-15

Hebrews 4:15-16

22. What are some practical ways you can live because of Jesus' ability to help? What prayers can you pray? What thoughts can you change? What actions can you take? (Use some of the help from question 21.)

23. Add the attributes of Jesus you have found in this lesson to the on-going "Jesus" list you began in Lesson 2.

MORE THAN MOSES

Hebrews 3

Jesus is the subject of the book of Hebrews. In this week's passage we will look closely at him, especially as he compares to the great hero of Judaism, Moses. Hebrews commends Moses as faithful leader of the house of God. And yet, it commends Jesus as the builder of the house. As we keep our focus on Jesus, we will keep from straying and from the danger that the people of Moses faced in the wilderness. Hebrews warns us that the dangers of unbelief, sin, hard-heartedness and disobedience that captured the people of Moses in the wilderness are still a threat.

Consider Jesus

1. The second chapter of Hebrews presents Jesus in both his deity and humanity. It also brings out what that means for those who believe. Use Hebrews 2:10-11 to flesh out the description of believers in Hebrews 3:1.

2. Starting in Hebrews 3:1 these "holy brethren" are asked again to "consider" Jesus. Look up the Greek word translated as "consider." What do you find out about this type of consideration?

3. One of the ways we are thinking intently and thoroughly about Jesus during this year of study is to keep a list (found in Lesson 2) of all that Hebrews says about the character, work and person of Jesus. Hebrews 3:1 adds apostle and high priest to that list. Jesus' high priesthood is a major theme of the book and we will spend several weeks on it later, so for now just look up the Greek word translated as "apostle." In what way is Jesus an "apostle of our confession"?

4. Again, Hebrews uses comparison and contrast to help us understand the superiority of Jesus. Make a list of all you see about both Moses and Jesus from Hebrews 3:2-6:

Moses   **Jesus**

5. How is Jesus like Moses and at the same time superior to Moses?

The Son in God's House

6. Throughout the comparison of Moses to Jesus, Hebrews refers to "God's house." What do you find out about "God's house" from Hebrews 3:2-6?

7. "God's house" is one of the many metaphors Scripture uses to explain the church. (Body, bride, holy nation etc.) To focus on the metaphor of "house" start by looking up the word translated as "house" or "household." What insights do you get?

8. Look up these references to the household or dwelling place of God. What additional truth do you gain from these "house" metaphors?

1 Corinthians 3:16-17; 6:19-20

Ephesians 2:19-22

1 Timothy 3:15

1 Peter 2:4-10

Hold Fast

9. At the end of Hebrews 3:6 it tells us that we are his house if we hold fast our confidence and our boasting in our hope. In Hebrews 3:14 it echoes the same idea, emphasizing "to the end." Scripture offers assurance of salvation to those with true faith, but it also warns against a version of so-called "faith" that doesn't bear fruit or last. Read Matthew 13:18-23. What are some kinds of incomplete faith?

10. "Continuance is the test of reality" when it comes to faith. Look up these other references to support this idea. How do continuing on in faith until death and assurance of salvation go hand in hand?

John 6:35-39

1 Corinthians 1:6-9

1 John 2:18-22

1 John 5:11-12

Take Care

11. Even with these assurances, Hebrews 3 contains a warning. Any good sermon contains illustrations. The illustration in Hebrews 3:7-11 is meant as a warning. Read Exodus 17:1-7 to get the original story. In what ways did the people in the wilderness fail in their faith and obedience? (You may want to look up the meanings of Meribah and Massah.)

12. The quote in Hebrews 3:7-11 comes from a psalm of David, which used the incident from Exodus as a warning to keep from becoming hard-hearted to the voice of God. Read Psalm 95:7-11. Summarize the warning in your own words.

13. Think of an experience of failure from your own life that either caused growth in your life or could serve as a warning to others. Tell a cautionary tale (a story of failure that teaches a positive lesson) from your life.

14. How can being willing to tell stories like these from your life warn others or help them to grow? What keeps us from using these kinds of life experiences in this way?

The Voice of God

15. It is interesting that the quote in Hebrews 3:7-11 is not ascribed to David. Who does verse 7 say is speaking in this passage? What does this imply about the voice behind Scripture?

16. How do we hear the voice of God today?

Hebrews 1:1-2

John 10:26-30

John 14:15-26

Hebrews 4:12

Warning

17. What actual warnings does the Spirit give in Hebrews 3:7-12? Think of at least three.

18. There is an action point in Hebrews 3:13. What does it mean to exhort one another? What would it take to be in relationships where this is possible? What is the difference between exhortation and criticism?

19. Read the exhortations in Ephesians 5:1-20 and Colossians 3:5-17. What further insights or action points do you gather about how accountability and encouragement work in the body of Christ?

20. Who in your life do you see in need of this type of encouragement? What could you do this week to help this person to keep from the deceitfulness of sin?

21. Why exhort others every day? Why do it in a timely manner (as the passage says "today")? What does this say about our vulnerability to sin? (1 Corinthians 10:12)

22. How do you know if *you* are becoming hard-hearted? What would be some signs? Really spend some time on this. Think about both practical answers and use these examples from Scripture: 2 Chronicles 36:11-16; Zechariah 7:8-14; Mark 3:1-6, 8:14-21.

23. Read through the questions and answers in Hebrews 3:16-19. What were the actions of those led by Moses? What does verse 19 say is the origin of those actions? Explain the connection between disobedience and unbelief.

24. The original recipients of this letter seem to have been tempted to fall away from Christ in unbelief. The writer reminds them that their forefathers failed at hearing, believing and obeying the voice of God as Moses led them. Have you been tempted to go back to the way you lived life before you came to faith? In what ways?

25. Think about an area in your life where you may be stiff-arming God even though you know what he has said? What evidence of unbelief may be in your heart? (Remember the evidences from questions 22 and 23.)

26. What practical steps can you take to restore or maintain a willing, believing heart toward the things of God?

27. What is the warning here to so-called "Christians" who may have made a profession of faith, but show no real change, obedience or fruit? What is the warning to those who acknowledge that they are unbelievers?

28. Remember to record all that you have learned about Jesus on the page in Lesson 2!

PROMISE OF REST

Hebrews 4:1-13

The Book of Hebrews continues the theme that God speaks in chapter four. The question is: what is God saying and what should the response be? According to this word from God the promise of rest still stands. Today, if anyone hears his voice, they must not harden their hearts to the "good news." Rather, when the "good news" is joined with faith, the one who receives the message enters a new kind of Sabbath rest. Let's learn what this means.

Rest

1. In our last lesson we left the concept of "rest" unexamined. Now we will take it on. Look up the word translated as "rest" in a Greek dictionary. What do you find?

2. There are at least two aspects to rest. One is the stoppage of work. The other is entering into a state of repose, blessing or peace. There are four examples of rest in Hebrews 3:15-4:10. For each try to identify what the "rest" entailed, whether or not the "rest " was entered, and how the "rest" is entered. Give verses for your answers. (If you have a hard time filling this in, do questions 3-8 and come back to this!)

	What Kind?	Entered (Y/N)	How?
Followers of Moses:			
Followers of Joshua:			
God after creation:			
Believers in the good news:			

3. OK, now that we have some familiarity with the passage, let's go back to Hebrews 4:1. The verse starts with "therefore." What truth from Hebrews 3:16-19 is the basis for what is next?

4. The rest of Hebrews 4:1 has both a promise and a caution. What are they?

5. In Hebrews 4:2, the phrase translated "good news" in the ESV is the Greek word "euaggelizo." (Strong's # 2097) What are some other ways this word is translated in other translations (such as NASB, NIV, KJV) of this passage? What are some of the ways it is used and translated in other passages within the Bible? What good news is this passage talking about?

Entering Rest

6. According to Hebrews 4:1-3 the fact that the "good news" has come and is heard by a person is not enough for that person to enter rest. What also has to happen? (See also Romans 10:8-17 for a more thorough answer.)

7. How does your answer to question six relate to the caution in Hebrews 4:1?

8. The history lesson from Hebrews 4 starts with creation. God rested from his work after creation. He offered rest in the Promised Land to the Jews whom he tested in the wilderness. They failed the test, languishing in unbelief and disobedience, and so failed to enter rest. Joshua did eventually lead the Jews into the land. Their rest was not the final rest this passage speaks of, though. We know this because David recounted the incident in the Psalms through the voice of the Holy Spirit and again offered rest. So there remains a rest. Hebrews 4:9-11 describes this new kind of rest. Use these cross-references to help define aspects of this rest:

Sabbath Rest:
Matthew 11:28-30

2 Timothy 4:7-8

1 Peter 1:3-5

Rested from his works:
Romans 4:2-6

Ephesians 2:8-9

Philippians 3:8-11

Revelation 14:12-13

9. Talk about the ways that believers experience rest for their souls now and also the way they will have perfect rest in the future. When have you experienced rest for your soul even in the midst of trial or hardship? Why?

10. Read Hebrews 4:11. How do we strive (or work) to enter rest?

    John 6:27-29

    Philippians 2:12-13

    Philippians 3:12-14

11. It seems like a paradox to work at faith. What are some ways that we can make an effort toward increasing faith? What have you done in the past that has helped your faith grow?

12. In the end of Hebrews 4:11, what was the "same sort of disobedience"? (Hebrews 3:18-19)

13. Sometimes as believers we can focus on the disobedience and sin of unbelievers hoping they will act better. Using the example of the Israelites in the wilderness, if their real problem wasn't just behavior, what was it? How would this change the way you interact with those who don't know Christ?

Today if You Hear

14. You have looked closely at the "rest" that is offered. When and how is the "rest" offered according to Hebrews 4:6-7?

15. Why is it important to respond to the voice of God "today"? What are the benefits of a quick response? What are the dangers of a delayed response?

16. Go back through Hebrews 4:1-8. Look for all the references to "hear," "hearing," "listening," and "speaking," "said," and "saying." What are they talking about; what "word" is the author exhorting his readers to hear?

Word of God

17. Now read Hebrews 4:12-13. In the context of all you saw in question 16, what is "the word of God" from Hebrews 4:12? (There are layers to this so don't be afraid to give several answers.)

18. Remember that as the writer quotes Scripture throughout Hebrews, he says that God (Father, Son, and Holy Spirit) has spoken it. In a sense, God's word exists in written form and yet it is still "heard." Relate this idea to the word being "living and active." How do the words of Scripture come alive to us?

19. Tell of the most recent time that God's word spoke directly and powerfully to your heart or circumstance.

20. When Hebrews 4:12 describes the precision and sharpness of God's word what does verse 12 say this discerns? What are the implications of this?

21. Sometimes we can deceive even ourselves with our rationalizations and excuses. We cannot fool God. How does God's word expose us? When has it exposed you?

22. Read Hebrews 4:13. Why is it sobering for unbelievers in this context? Why is it also sobering for believers? What action does it inspire?

23. Remember that God's word is not a text that we just master as if it were an academic subject. *It is the voice of God that masters us.* So, what is your regular practice of reading, meditating on, and responding to the voice of God in his word? How can you open yourself up to the action of God's word in your life?

24. Record anything new that you have learned about Jesus on the page in Lesson 2.

THE HIGH PRIEST OF GRACE

Hebrews 4:14-5:10

The high priesthood of Jesus is a major theme of the book of Hebrews. Jesus' role as high priest is a multifaceted gem and we will explore it deeply in later lessons. For now, we will focus in on one of the most beautiful and practical facets of the gem. Jesus's high priesthood is rooted in his human experience and provides for us an unprecedented example of sinless life. It also opens up a new access to the throne of God to receive mercy and grace for our many needs.

High Priests

1. In Hebrews chapters 7-10 it gives a detailed explanation of Jesus' high priesthood. This week's lesson will seem like we are just touching on some details but don't worry, we will cover them in the coming weeks. Let's start in Hebrews 5:1-4. List everything you learn about the high priests.

2. In what ways is Jesus like the Old Testament high priests? How is Jesus different from the O.T. priests? (From Hebrews 4:14- 5:5-6.)

3. In Hebrews 4:14 it tells us that Jesus, the Son of God, "passed through the heavens." Look up Hebrews 1:3, 8:1-5 and 9:23-24. What did Jesus pass through the heavens to do? Why is Jesus' sacrifice as a high priest so important as we "hold fast our confession"?

In Temptation

4. In Hebrews 5:1-3 it reinforces that because a human high priest is "chosen from among men," he is also a sinner, so he can understand and deal gently with other people's sins. He offers gifts and sacrifices to God for both his sins and the sins of the people. How does his own sinfulness help him to "deal gently" with others?

5. In Hebrews 4:15 it tells us that Jesus is also able to sympathize with our weakness. What makes him able to sympathize? What is different about Jesus' sympathy compared to a high priest's?

6. How sympathetic are you when others around you sin? Why? What is the difference between sympathy that helps someone overcome their sin and sympathy that enables their sin to continue?

7. Let's spend some time looking at some of the temptation Jesus faced when he was a man. Read Matthew 4:1. Who was behind the temptations Jesus faced? What part did the Spirit play?

8. The word translated as "tested" or "tempted" in Matthew 4:1; Hebrews 4:15 and Hebrews 11:17 is the Greek word *"peirazo"*. It is used for both "tempting to evil," and for "testing of faith" or "testing to prove the quality" of something. So, it can have a negative or positive meaning depending on the motivations of the tester or tempter. Use this information to help you add to your answer for question 6. In James 1:13-15 it adds more to the discussion of the origins of temptation. What else do you learn?

9. Now read Matthew 4:1-11. List and describe how Jesus was tempted. What circumstances added to the power of the temptation?

10. Given the power of a direct encounter with Satan, Jesus' hunger, the fact that he was alone in a wilderness and the enticements of the actual offers of Satan, how has Jesus been tempted in all the ways we are tempted? Read also I John 2:15-17.

11. How did Jesus combat the temptation? Relate this back to what you just studied in Hebrews 4:12-13.

12. What scriptures would help you combat a temptation that you often face? Name the temptation and write out the scripture here. Consider memorizing this verse!

13. Have you noticed that when you do not give in to temptation, that in that moment you experience greater depths of struggle, even pain? Conversely, when you give in quickly, the temptation brings the pleasure of sin rather than pain of self-control? How does Jesus' sinless life help him to sympathize with this struggle in a way that other high priests can't?

Jesus Prays

14. In Hebrews 5:7-10 it describes another circumstance in Jesus' life when he faced great temptation. Read Matthew 26:36-46. What temptation did Jesus face at this time in his life? Was it easy to submit to God's will in this circumstance? How do you know? Read also Luke 22:44.

15. Now look at Hebrews 5:7. What was God able to do in this circumstance? Did God hear Jesus' request?

16. To start to understand God's answer to Jesus' prayer in the garden, look up the Greek words translated as "learned" in Hebrews 5:8 and "perfect" in Hebrews 5:9. What do you find out?

17. Based on Hebrews 5:8-9, what was God's answer to Jesus' prayers, and why did he answer that way?

18. When we pray that God's will is done, does this mean that there will always be comfortable outcomes for us? How can this knowledge deepen our prayers and open our eyes to the ways God sometimes works through pain?

Draw Near

19. Now let's go back to Hebrews 4:16. Look up the Greek word translated "confidence." What do you find out about the attitude we can take when we approach God with our weaknesses, needs and temptations? Why can we have this boldness?

20. How can this invitation change the way you pray? What do you need to speak openly with God about today?

21. When we draw near to his throne, we see that the throne is a "throne of grace." What are we offered at this throne according to Hebrews 4:16? Notice that this is not a throne of judgment!

22. What is the difference between mercy and grace? How do they complement one another in helping us? Look these words up if you need help.

23. One of the much-neglected ideas contained in "grace" is that it is God's power available for the Christian to live out the Christian life. Grace doesn't just cover our sins; *it empowers us to do what is right*. What are some of the methods that God uses to give us the power to do what is right in our time of need? Think of at least three and connect your answers with scriptures.

24. Compare what you have learned in this lesson about testing, completeness, and asking for wisdom to James 1:2-5. What are some action points?

25. Go boldly to the throne of grace for some need in your life right now. Write out your prayer here.

26. Log any new things you have learned about Jesus on the page in Lesson 2.

THE DANGER OF DULLNESS

Hebrews 5:11-6:12
Hebrews 10:26-31

This is one of the most difficult sections in the New Testament to interpret. We approach it humbly, knowing that godly men and women may disagree. Yet, we know this truth is God's truth, so we seek to unlock the very strong warning this passage contains: Not everyone who is in the midst of a group of believers has really obtained salvation through grace by faith. Some have grown dull to the truth that surrounds them and have not moved all the way to saving faith. For those who "taste" but never truly "eat," there is a great danger of becoming so immune to the beginnings of the truth they already know, that they turn completely away from Jesus, the one that the truth points toward. They give up on Jesus and don't believe in him as the savior. In a way, then, they participate again in his crucifixion by approving of it and opening Jesus to the shame of it all over again. What a warning!

Background Information

Before we get started on this passage it is a good idea to review the context of this letter and thus this passage. This letter to the Hebrews was written after Jesus had risen from the dead and there had been enough time for the word to spread. (After 35 A.D.) Apparently, enough time had passed that the author was expecting these Hebrews to exhibit true faith that was enduring. However, remember the New Testament Scriptures were not yet compiled so these Jews had very little to go on as they considered, believed and matured in Christianity. Judaism was familiar and was still being practiced around them. The animal sacrificial system was still in place, the Temple was still standing. (Before 70 A.D.) It seems that some were in danger of holding to the old religious practices even as they acknowledged Jesus as "the Christ." Beyond this, those around them that continued to practice Judaism now considered them unclean and subjected them to persecution and ostracism. So, there was a temptation to return to the Judaism they knew, or to treat Jesus as an "add-on." In the relatively short thirty-five year span we are talking about, it is easy to see how confusing this may have been for the Hebrew people.

The letter extensively developed the theme of Jesus' priesthood and how he abolished the sacrificial system to correct this error and confusion. The Hebrew people were exhorted to embrace the full meaning of Christ's sacrifice and it was argued over and over that Jesus was better than any of the ways their forefathers had worshiped. They may have been deprived of the old ways, but Jesus was superior in every way. They were exhorted again and again to persevere in their faith and were warned against turning away from Jesus and back to their old religious system. Jesus was presented as great high priest; there was no other. There was no turning back!

Dull

1. Read Hebrews 5:11-14. The writer leaves behind his discussion of Jesus as "the high priest after the order of Melchizedek" (which he will resume in chapter 7) in order to interject this warning. He starts by telling them they are "dull." Look up the Greek word translated as "dull." What is the definition, and what seems to be the basis of their immaturity?

2. What are the three marks of maturity that Hebrews 5:12-14 mentions? Immaturity? Just name them for now.

3. Look up Acts 7:38 and Romans 3:2. What do these verses say that Jews would have considered "the oracles of God"? With this in mind, are "the oracles of God" mentioned here the gospel of Jesus?

4. To get a fuller picture of the purpose of "the oracles" or the "the law" read Galatians 3:21-24. Why would it have been important for these Hebrews to know the basics of the Old Testament? To what and to whom do they point?

Leaving the Old

5. The "word of righteousness" and "solid food" point to the true gospel of salvation in Jesus. Use Romans 10:1-4 to explain the relationship between the law and the gospel.

6. In Hebrews 6:1-2 it tells the Hebrews to leave the basic doctrine of Christ. The Greek word translated "leave" means to forsake, let alone, disregard, or put away. This gives us a big clue as to what the writer is asking his audience to "mature" away from. Nowhere in Scripture are we told to sever ourselves from the basics of the gospel. We are to build on them, celebrate them, and remember them. So, these people are most likely not being asked to just move on from the basics of Christianity. Fill in these blanks to see what is missing in their "beginning doctrine."

These Old Testament truths:
- Repentance from dead works (Hosea 14:1-2)
- Faith toward God (Habakkuk 2:4; Genesis 15:6)
- Instructions about (ritual) washings (Leviticus 15:11-13; Numbers 19)
- Laying on of hands (Leviticus 4:1-4, 16:21-22)
- Resurrection of the dead (Daniel 12:2)
- Eternal judgment (Isaiah 66:24)

Are transformed into these New Testament truths:

- Repentance from: _____ Luke 5:32

- Faith in: _____ Acts 20:21

- Instructions about the washing of: _____ Titus 3:5

  And the washing of: _____ 1 Peter 3:21

- Instead of laying hands on a sacrificial animal we place our sin on:

  _____ 1 Peter 2:24

- Resurrection of _____ John 11:25

- Release from _____ John 5:24

7. In light of all of this, why would the Hebrew people need to leave behind or sever themselves from their beginning understanding of Christ? (Hebrews 6:1)

8. Have you had an experience with a person who has "faith in God" but does not accept Jesus? What do you think stops people at this point? How can you help them make the connection between what they already believe to faith in Jesus?

Mature Faith

9. Now let's go back to the descriptions of the mature in Hebrews 5:11-14 from Question 2. Evaluate yourself by these marks of mature faith.

10. What can you do to cultivate this type of faith? What can you do to "have your powers of discernment trained by constant practice"? (Hebrews 5:14)

Assurance of Salvation

11. Now read Hebrews 6:4-6. There are three main interpretations of this passage.

1. A true believer can fall away and lose his salvation.
2. This is given as a hypothetical, yet impossible, warning for immature Christians to challenge them to persevere.
3. This describes a person who has had much exposure and maybe even enthusiasm for Christ, but in the end, he stubbornly rejects the gospel.

An important principle in Bible interpretation is to avoid creating a doctrine on a single passage. Instead we use Scripture to interpret Scripture and look for the bulk of evidence to support a doctrine. We also interpret unclear Scripture in light of clear Scripture. Scripture teaches in multiple places that once a person truly repents of his sin and believes in Jesus as the payment for his sin that person is given salvation by grace through faith. It also teaches that salvation is secure because of the power of God and the surety of his promises. Use these passages to support this doctrine and to evaluate the first interpretation given above.

1 John 5:6-13

1 Peter 1:3-5

Titus 3:4-7

Colossians 3:3

Philippians 1:6

Ephesians 2:5-9

2 Corinthians 5:1-8

Romans 8:31-39

John 10:27-29

Warning

Remember the context as we return to our passage in Hebrews 4:4-6. The writer is warning those who are tempted to hold only to an elementary but not saving view of Christ. He is warning them against an "immature," thus incomplete, faith. He is in the process of reminding them of the superiority of Christ in every way. Some of these Hebrew people are on the brink of embracing the mature, complete view of the gospel of Jesus that he is arguing for but some, in their dullness, are in danger of heading back to the known entity of Judaism. He wants to make sure they know the dire consequences of leaving Jesus behind and not embracing the fullness of the gospel.

12. Use each phrase from Hebrews 6:4-5 to describe how a person can experience some of God without really placing their faith in Christ as savior.

Example:

Enlightened: A person can truly understand the gospel or "be enlightened" without actually believing.

Tasted the heavenly gift:
(Contrast John 4:10)

Shared in the Holy Spirit:
(Contrast 1 Corinthians 6:19)

Tasted the goodness of the word of God:
(Contrast Jeremiah 15:16; John 6:51)

And the powers of the age to come:
(Powers of the age to come most likely refers to miracles)

13. The person described here is poised to come to full faith. The next step would be to fully embrace Jesus, to stop tasting and drink and eat fully. Read Romans 10 again and explain how this could happen.

14. The alternative to being saved is falling away. If this person falls away, in what way is it impossible to restore this person to repentance? What does the passage say this person is doing to the Son of God? Also read Hebrews 10:26 to add to your answer.

15. What is the warning for these Hebrews on the verge of either true faith or return to Judaism? Read Hebrews 10:27-31 as well to add to your answer.

16. There is a strong warning in Hebrews 6 and Hebrews 10. How can you take this warning seriously if you or someone you know is in the process of turning away from faith?

Two Options

17. Hebrews 6:7-8 gives an illustration of the two ways that the Hebrews could go with the "rain" they have so far. What does the field that produces a useful crop represent? How does a true believer "drink in rain"? How does he "produce a crop"?

18. What does the second field produce? What is its end? How about the person this field represents, what does he produce and what is his end?

Sure of Better Things

19. In Hebrews 6:9 notice the pronoun shift. In Hebrews 6:4-6 the people are referred to as "those" and "them." Now who is being addressed? What other descriptor is used for this group?

20. In Hebrews 6:9-12 what is the assurance given? What makes the author sure of things that belong to salvation? What part of that surety is based on God and what part is based on them?

21. Attach Hebrews 6:12 to Hebrews 5:11. (The words translated as "dull" and "sluggish" are the same Greek word.)

22. How is it possible to have "full assurance and hope until the end"? In light of all that you have studied, what do *you* need to do to have this assurance?

23. Log any new insights about the salvation Jesus offers on the page in Lesson 2.

THE PROMISE

Hebrews 6:12-20

As a follow up to the warning against rejecting Christ, the writer to the Hebrews writes one of the strongest passages in all of Scripture about the assurance of salvation. He reminds us that God gave his promise to Abraham and this sure promise finds its ultimate fulfillment in Christ. Because God's promises are absolutely sure (he is unable to lie!), we can rest in the high priestly work of Jesus as an anchor for our soul. That anchor is as sure as the promise of God!

Assurance of God's Promise

1. Read Hebrews 6:9-20. Last lesson we affirmed that the person who has truly believed in Jesus can be sure of their salvation. The passage we will study in this lesson builds on this. Look back to Hebrews 6:10-12. What gives the author assurance of salvation for his "beloved" brothers and sisters?

2. In Hebrews 6:13-20 it gives an even stronger assurance, the assurance of God's promise. The author goes all the way back to Abraham as an example. Read the following passages and record how they chronicle God's promise to Abraham.

Genesis 12:1-4

Genesis 15:1-6

Genesis 17:1-8

Genesis 17:15-21

Genesis 21:1-13

Genesis 22:1-18

3. In Genesis 22:16 God swears by himself, why did he do this according to Hebrews 6:13, 16-17? How was this oath for Abraham and also for those who would later inherit his promise?

4. In Hebrews 6:15 it says that Abraham patiently waited and obtained the promise. What promise did he obtain? Describe the ways he was patient.

5. Describe how Abraham was also impatient with the promises of God. Why do you think this isn't mentioned in Hebrews?

6. Sometimes we think that when we fail to be perfectly patient and faithful God can't use us. What encouragement does Abraham's example give us?

7. Part of the promise that God made to Abraham is found in Genesis 22:18. What is the promise and who is Abraham's offspring? Use Galatians 3:15-18 to answer.

8. Did Abraham see this promise fulfilled? What does this say about the timing of God's promises and the necessity of faith and patience for those who trust God's promises?

9. Think of an example (either past or present) when your circumstances called for patience with the promises of God. When have you had to walk by faith not knowing the exact outcome of your trust in God?

10. Who will inherit the promises that Abraham did not live to see fulfilled? Use Galatians 3:23-29 and Romans 4:13-25 to help you answer.

11. Remember the writer is in the middle of a digression. He wants to make sure his audience is secure in their faith before he tries to teach them the depths of Jesus' high priesthood. What, then, are the two unchangeable things of Hebrews 6:18?

12. Read Hebrews 6:19. How would the fact that God is unable to lie give the Hebrews security?

Refuge and Anchor

13. In Hebrews 6:18 it says some have "fled for refuge." There are at least two ways we flee for refuge to God. The first is for salvation. Tell the story again of how you first realized you needed a savior for your sins.

14. A second way we flea for refuge is in the midst of spiritual need. Tell of a time when you have "fled for refuge" to God. How has God met you in your need? What part did the security of your salvation play in your ability to trust him? What part did his "inability to lie" or the truth of God's word play?

15. In Hebrews 6:19-20 it describes an anchor of the soul. What is this anchor? Use also Psalm 110:4 and Hebrews 5:6.

16. In Hebrews 6:19-20 it tells us that Jesus is the anchor of our soul because he entered behind the curtain, because he went as a forerunner, and because he is a high priest forever. When we get to Hebrews 9 we will look at Jesus entering the inner place behind the curtain in depth. For now, look up Numbers 18:1-7; Matthew 27:45-51 and Hebrews 9:1-3,11-12 to explain Hebrews 6:19. What curtain did Jesus enter and why?

17. In what way is Jesus our forerunner, or in what ways has he gone ahead of us to secure a place? Use Hebrews 6:19-20, 12:2 and John 13:36, 14:1-3 to help explain.

18. Let's go back to the concept of an anchor. What does an anchor do for a ship in a calm sea? What does an anchor do for a ship in a stormy sea? What does an anchor need on the floor of a sea to get a firm hold? How heavy does an anchor need to be to really hold?

19. What kind of problems or temptations were the Hebrews facing? (Hebrews 3:12-13; 4:1; 5:11; 10:25, 33,34.) How does this idea of an anchor help them?

20. When the storms of doubt, persecution, or hard life circumstances come, how is Jesus an anchor for your soul? What can you do to cling to this anchor in a storm? Think of at least three things you can do!

21. It is also true that we need an anchor to keep us from drifting from the centrality of Christ in our lives. Are there areas in your life that you anchor in self or others rather than in Christ? Any areas where your agenda takes first place? Why do you think this is a temptation?

22. How do you know if you are drifting? What can you do to anchor yourself during the regular flow of life? Is this different than anchoring for a storm?

23. Read through Hebrews 6:13-20. By way of summary, what is God's promise, and how do we know the promise is trustworthy?

24. Log the things that you have learned about Jesus on the list in Lesson 2.

THE HIGHEST PRIEST

Hebrews 7

Now the author begins the central section of The Letter to the Hebrews. He reveals Jesus as high priest in great detail over the next four chapters. By explaining the origins of Jesus' priesthood to his Jewish audience, he helps them see his superiority to the Levitical priesthood. He sets Jesus up as a priest "after the order of Melchizedek." Let's find out what this means.

Melchizedek

1. Hebrews 7 continues what the author started in Hebrews 4:14-5:10 and Hebrews 6:19-20. Review these passages. Now read Hebrews 7:1-3. Make a list of all the things you learn about Melchizedek:

2. So far in this letter, the author has sought to prove that Jesus is better by way of contrast. Here he uses comparison. From Hebrews 7:1-3 list all the ways Jesus is like Melchizedek:

Melchizedek
Ex.: King of the Most High God

Jesus
King of the Kingdom of God

3. Look up Isaiah 9:6-7 and Jeremiah 23:5-6; note these prophetic titles of the Messiah. How did Melchizedek's priesthood foreshadow or create a "type" of these titles while Jesus is the fulfillment?

4. Let's get to know Melchizedek better. Read Genesis 14:17-20. This is the only story in the Old Testament describing the life of Melchizedek. In Hebrews 7:3 it says that he had no genealogy and is without father or mother. In light of how little we know about him, most commentators say because no genealogy is recorded, though he had parents, we just don't know who they are. It also isn't recoded when he was born or died. This makes him seem like someone who has no "beginning of days" nor "end of life." How does Jesus have neither a beginning of days nor end of life?

5. In Hebrews 7:4 it asks the Jewish reader to consider the greatness of Melchizedek. What is the evidence of his greatness given in each of these verses:

Hebrews 7:4

Hebrews 7:6

Hebrews 7:7

Hebrews 7:8

Hebrews 7:9-10

A New Way of Thinking

6 How do you think this comparison of Abraham (and Levi) with Melchizedek would have struck the Jewish readers of the day? Would it have been easy to change the way they thought about Abraham?

7. When have you had to rethink your position on something given new or better thinking? Are you open to change or resistant to it? How might this play into how likely you are to change in light of what you learn in Scripture?

8. It is also true that in church circles we can hold very tightly to "the way we do it." Ponder the value of tradition in Christianity versus the value of being open to new methods and practices of Christianity. What are the risks and benefits of both? How do we evaluate traditions?

Levitical Priesthood

9. The author of Hebrews challenges another strongly held religious institution, the Levitical priesthood, in Hebrews 7:11-20. Start with Hebrews 7:11, 18-19. In what ways were the Levitical priesthood and the law it represented deficient? (See also Romans 3:19-21)

10. In Hebrews 7:12-14 the author points out that the change in priesthood must also include a change in the law about priesthood. According to the law how did a priest become a priest? (Exodus 28:1 and 29:1-9)

11. According to Hebrews 7:13-14 how is Jesus' priesthood different from the Levitical priesthood? What tribe is Jesus from?

12. In Hebrews 7:15-17 the author quotes the prophetic Psalm 110:4. How do these verses explain the nature and basis of Jesus' priesthood?

A Superior Priesthood

13. In Hebrews 7:20-21 it harkens back to Hebrews 6:16-17. What was another evidence that this priesthood is a superior priesthood? How reliable is God's oath?

14. The author really makes a strong case for Jesus' superiority as the high priest of a better covenant. Read Hebrews 7:23-28. List every description of Jesus' priesthood.

15. Why can't Levitical priests live up to this description? List their limitations.

To the Uttermost

16. Go back to Hebrews 7:25. What does it mean that Jesus saves to the "uttermost"? See what you learn from these references:

Philippians 1:6

Colossians 1:11-14

1 Peter 1:3-5

1 Peter 2:9-10

2 Peter 1:3-4

17. Jesus saves us through grace by faith as we repent and place our trust in him as payment for our sins. This is justification. He continues work out our salvation as he transforms our character into Christlikeness throughout our lives. This is sanctification. He will complete our salvation eventually through our eternal reward in heaven. This is glorification. All three of these are parts being saved to the "uttermost." Write out a prayer here thanking Jesus for his "uttermost" salvation.

Makes Intercession

18. To see how Jesus lives to make intercession (Hebrews 7:25), look up the following verses and note what you learn.

Romans 8:27

Romans 8:34

1 Timothy 2:5

1 John 2:1

19. In John 17:6-26 we hear Jesus making intercession by praying for us. This prayer is often titled "The High Priestly Prayer." What does he pray for? List as many things as you can.

20. Go back and read this passage and substitute your name when Jesus uses the words "they" or "them." What impact does this prayer have on you emotionally? What assurance does this prayer give you?

21. Go back to the "Jesus" page in Lesson 2. Log in all that you have learned about Jesus, our great high priest of the order of Melchizedek. Spend some time in praise and worship!

THE SUPERIORITY OF THE SON

Hebrews 8

Jesus is our great high priest. One of the things Jesus does as high priest is mediate a new covenant. The old covenant gave the standards of God and demonstrated his righteousness. It also showed our sin. The new covenant is not a remake of the old! It is enacted on better promises, and Hebrews 8 teaches us that it is better in so many ways. One of the most astounding ways it is better is that it actually changes our hearts!

In the True Tent

1. Hebrews 8:1 presents "the point" of what has been said so far. Review Hebrews 7:23-28. When the author says we have "such a high priest" what attributes is he recalling?

2. Read Hebrews 8:1-6. According to these verses where is Jesus and what is he doing?

3. We will learn much more about the tabernacle or tent as we study Hebrews 9 but for now, describe the relationship between the tabernacle on earth and the tabernacle in heaven. Which came first? What was the purpose of the earthly tent? (Hebrews 8:1-2,5)

4. The tent in heaven and the tent on earth are different, but so are the sacrifices made in them. What sets Jesus' sacrifice apart from the earthly priests' sacrifices? Why couldn't Jesus be another earthly priest? (Hebrews 8:3-4, 6)

Mediator

5. In Hebrews 8:6 it presents Jesus' ministry as the mediator of the new covenant. Let's begin to understand this ministry by looking up the Greek word translated as "mediator." What do you learn about Jesus?

6. Look up these verses to help you understand Jesus as mediator. What do you learn?

Hebrews 8:6

Hebrews 9:15

Hebrews 12:24

1 Timothy 2:5-6

7. In Colossians 1:15-22 it gives a beautiful description of Jesus' work as mediator. What has Jesus reconciled as our mediator?

Old Covenant

Before we look at the better covenant and the better promises of Hebrews 8, let's look at the old covenant referred to here. There are many covenants that God made with the patriarchs (Noah, Abraham, Moses, David) in the Old Testament. This passage leads us to focus primarily on one such covenant. Turn to Exodus 19:5. In Exodus 19:5-6 God makes a covenant with Israel through Moses. God then gives the Ten Commandments and the rest of the law (Exodus 20-24). After he gives the law Moses confirms the covenant in Exodus 24:5-8. Then God calls Moses onto the mountain and writes the law on tablets of stone in Exodus 24:12.

8. What was the promise of the Mosaic covenant? What were the conditions? (Exodus 19:5-6) Did the people keep their end of the covenant? (Think about the whole history of Israel.)

9. Next the writer of Hebrews quotes Jeremiah 31:31-34 to introduce a new covenant and to evaluate the old covenant. From Hebrews 8:7-9, what is the "fault" with the old covenant?

10. If the law of the old covenant was so easily broken, then why establish this covenant and have laws? In Romans 3:1-25 Paul responds to this question. The law of the old covenant was given to show something about Israel, God, mankind's sin, and Jesus. Use these verses from Romans 3 to flesh out the usefulness of the old covenant. What is revealed about each of these?

The Jews (Romans 3:1-3,9)

God (Romans 3:3-6; 21-22; 25)

Mankind and Sin (Romans 3:9-20,23)

Jesus (Romans 3:22,24-25)

Old vs. New

11. Let's look at the way that the new covenant (that Jeremiah prophesied and Jesus mediated as high priest) is better. Compare the Old and new covenants on this chart using Hebrews 8:9-13.

Verse	Old	New
8:9	Conditional	
8:10	Law written on tablets	
8:11	Taught by others	
8:12	Sins covered temporarily	
8:13	Obsolete	

12. This new covenant is not based on the condition of man's obedience, but on the promises of God. Write the "I will" statements from Hebrews 8:8-13. What difference does it make that God promises these things?

13. One of the important parts of the new covenant is the promise of a renewed heart. (Hebrews 8:10) Another prophecy from Ezekiel helps us understand the promise of a new heart. Read Ezekiel 36:25-27. List the "I will" statements that God makes in this passage.

14. Connect Ezekiel to John 14:15-26. What promises does Jesus give us to fulfill this prophecy? How is obedience (of a Christian) the *result* of the new covenant, not a *condition* like the old covenant?

15. Paul also contrasts the old and new covenants in 2 Corinthians 3:4-18. Go through this passage slowly, phrase by phrase, and write a list of the effects of the new covenant on a believer's life.

Heart Transformation

16. The idea of a transformed heart is all through the New Testament. It is one of the great truths of the gospel. The law could never change our hearts. Heart and life change are only possible through Christ. Look up these passages and rephrase them as a new covenant promise or truth.

Galatians 2:20: When I believed in Jesus, my old self died. Now Christ actually lives in me! Faith in Jesus changes my life from the inside.

John 3:3

Romans 6:4-6

2 Corinthians 5:17

Galatians 4:4-7

Galatians 5:22-25

Ephesians 4:22-24

Philippians 2:12-13

Colossians 3:10-11

1 John 5:1-3

17. In Hebrews 8:11 it assures us that we can know God intimately and that he knows us. He is very involved with each believer to bring about change. Tell a story of how God has changed your heart. When did you respond to a circumstance or person in a redeemed way because of what Christ is doing to change you?

18. Heart change begins at the initial moment of salvation, but it also continues throughout life and will continue until it is perfected in heaven. (Philippians 1:6) Take some time to pray and ask Jesus to continue his work in you in a certain area of your life. Write the prayer as a journal entry here:

19. There is a great assurance in Hebrews 8:12. While God is in the process of knowing, changing and redeeming us, what is also true? How is that different from the old covenant?

20. What does it mean to you that God is merciful and won't remember your sins? What freedom does this give you? How does this change the way you think about your sin?

21. Log all that you have learned about Jesus on the page in Lesson 2.

THE TABERNACLE

Hebrews 9:1-14

The tabernacle and eventually the temple were central to Jewish religious life from the time of Moses all the way to the time of Christ's coming. All of the Jewish people would have been familiar with the furnishings of the tabernacle and the rituals and sacrifices performed within it. They understood the fundamental importance of sacrifice in their relationship to God. It was so fundamental to their religious life that it was hard for them to give it up. The writer to the Hebrews uses this center section of his letter to make clear that Jesus is the final and ultimate sacrifice for sin. This reality changes worship for all time! The place to start in building his argument is in the tabernacle, so we will also start by understanding the tabernacle and its place in the old covenant.

The Tabernacle

1. In Hebrews 9:1 it tells us that the old covenant had regulations for worship and an earthly place of holiness. In verse 2 it tells us that this earthly place was a tent or tabernacle. Look up the Greek word translated as "tent" in the ESV. What do you learn? According to Exodus 25:8, what was the purpose of this tent?

2. In Exodus 25-27 it records the original instructions for the furnishings of the tabernacle named in Hebrews 9. Look up each of these and write a *very brief* description. (You don't need to include every detail. We are just getting familiar with them.)

The Tent
(Exodus 26)

Lampstand
(Exodus 25:31-40)

The Table and the Bread of The Presence
(Exodus 25:23-30)

The Second Curtain (The Veil)
(Exodus 26:31-33)

The Golden Altar of Incense
(Exodus 30:1-10)

The Ark of the Covenant
(Exodus 25:10-16)

Golden Jar of Manna
(Exodus 16:32-34)

Aaron's Staff
(Numbers 17:8-10)

Tablets of the Covenant
(Exodus 31:18; 32:15-16)

Mercy Seat with The Golden Cherubim
(Exodus 25:17-21)

3. Remember that the instructions for all the things that you just described were given directly by God to Moses. What do you think these instructions for the dwelling place of God were meant to tell the people about God? (Think in terms of the authority of God, how approachable he is, his glory, his holiness, man's sin, etc.)

4. Why do you think the instructions were so precise? What would this have inspired in the worshiper?

5. After what was the tabernacle patterned? (Hebrews 8:1-5) What does this add to the reason for the precision in the instructions for the tabernacle?

6. How we worship also says something about what we believe about God. Think about the way that you approach worship. What does your most common method of worship reveal about what you think about the holiness and approachability of God? (There may be positive and negative aspects to this. Try to think of both!)

Ritual Duties

7. In Hebrews 9:6 it tells us that priests go regularly into the first section to perform "ritual duties." (You would need to study all of Leviticus to describe these duties. Don't panic, we're not going to do it!) These regular ritual sacrifices are contrasted with the Day of Atonement (Hebrews 9:7.) Read Leviticus 16. What is the Day of Atonement? How is it different from the other ritual sacrifices?

8. The author of Hebrews doesn't need to go into all of these details because his audience is very familiar with them. (Hebrews 9:5) According to Hebrews 9:8-10 what are the deficiencies of these rituals and sacrifices. (Name at least four from this passage.)

9. What is the "time of reformation" from Hebrews 9:10? Use a word study of the Greek word translated as "reformation" and the context of the passage to answer.

Great High Priest

10. All of this sets up the author's presentation of Jesus as the Great High Priest again. Read Hebrews 9:11-14 and fill in the chart below:

Old Covenant	Jesus
Created, earthly, patterned tent	
High priest enters most holy place	
By means of blood of goats and calves	
Temporary offerings	
Purification of the flesh	
Cannot perfect the conscience	

11. What does the work of Jesus do for us according to Hebrews 9:12 and 9:14? How would these statements have affected the Hebrews to whom the letter was written? How does it give them encouragement to leave their old religious ways and to stand up under persecution?

12. We have already studied the security of our eternal redemption in depth (in Lessons 7 and 8) and the change of heart that the new covenant brings (in Lesson 10). Remember those lessons and look up the following verses. What does it mean to have our conscience purified (or cleansed) from dead works?

Romans 7:4

Ephesians 5:25-27

Colossians 2:12-13

Titus 2:14

1 John 1:7-10

13. What does Hebrews 9:14 say this purification frees us to do? Look up the Greek word translated as "serve" in the ESV for help.

Worship

14. How does our purified (cleansed) conscience lead us to deeper, more personal worship? (See also Hebrews 4:16 and 7:19.) What are some worship responses that could come from this for you? (Example: thanksgiving)

15. In Romans 12:1 it describes worship in another way. Paraphrase each of these phrases from the verse to help expand your view of worship.

By the mercies of God

Present your bodies

A living sacrifice

Holy and acceptable to God

Which is your spiritual worship

16. With all of this in mind, how can you more effectively worship and serve the living God?

17. If all of life can express worship, what area of your life is the least worshipful now? How can you change this into an expression of worship? Think of this in very practical terms.

18. Add anything new you learned about Jesus to the list in Lesson 2. This may be a good time to stop and worship!

THE BLOOD SACRIFICE

Hebrews 9:15-10:19

In this section of Hebrews, the author answers a very important question for the Jewish readers: Why did the Messiah have to die? Jews of this time had the idea of a triumphant, ruling, Messiah in their theology — not a suffering, dying, sacrificial savior. Therefore, it was just as crucial to explore the meaning of Jesus' death as it was to explore his role as eternal high priest. Amazingly, Jesus is not just the high priest of a new covenant; he is also the sacrifice of the new covenant!

High Priest and Sacrifice

1. We will look at Hebrews 9:15-28 in detail over the course of this lesson. To start, let's explore Jesus' role as both the *high priest* and *the sacrifice*. Review Hebrews 9:11-14 and read Hebrews 9:15-28. Note each time the passages describe Jesus as either of these two:

High Priest   **Sacrifice**

2. What do you see in Hebrews 9:15 that explains both of the roles you explored in the chart above? What is the result for "those who are called"?

3. Look up the Greek word translated as "redeems" (ESV). What (who) specifically is redeemed and how?

The Blood

4. In Hebrews 9:15-22 the writer connects blood and death with the inauguration of covenants. The first example he gives is about human inheritances. (The Greek word translated as "will" here is translated "covenant" in the rest of the passage.) In Hebrews 9:16-17 what is the writer's point?

5. In Hebrews 9:18-20 he gives another example of death, blood and the inauguration of a covenant. Read Exodus 24:3-8. Who made the sacrifice? Whose blood was used in this case? Why does the writer of Hebrews use this example? Would his original readers have been familiar with this example? (Hebrews 9:18)

6. Later, after the tabernacle was erected and the sacrificial system was in place, many sacrifices would be made. (Leviticus 4-7) According to Hebrews 9:21-22, what are the effects of these sacrifices?

7. According to Leviticus 17:11 why is blood so important? How does Hebrews 9:22 affirm this?

8. The author again emphasizes Jesus' sacrifice of himself as better than any previous sacrifice, while affirming the principle that blood must be shed and a life must be given for the forgiveness of sin. Go through Hebrews 9:23-26, 10:1-4 and 10:11-14 phrase by phrase and list the ways that Jesus' sacrifice is the better (perfect) sacrifice for sin.

9. What do you think the impact of this list would have been on the Jewish readers of the day who were wavering in their new Christianity?

The Father's Will

10. In Hebrews 10:5-10 it also brings out the important point that Jesus was doing the Father's will. What was the Father's will according to Hebrews 10:5-10? (Find at least 3 things!) Was this easy for Jesus? How do you know?

11. Jesus is the perfect example of making it his life's mission to do the will of the Father no matter what it took. Look up these verses and begin to think through what the "will of the Father" is for you. How are you responding to his will? (John 6:40; Romans 12:2; Ephesians 6:6-7; 1 Thessalonians 5:12-18)

12. Blood sacrifice sounds odd to our modern ears, but to the Jews of Jesus' day it was absolutely integral to their understanding of their relationship with God. Jesus taught his disciples directly about this new covenant and about his flesh and blood sacrifice. Read John 6:49-58 and observe the text closely. Pull out all that Jesus teaches about his flesh and blood.

13. Jesus was completely aware that his death and resurrection were the central purpose of the Father's will for his life. Read these statements that Jesus made and summarize what Jesus taught about himself.

John 2:18-22

John 10:17-18

Mark 8:31

Mark 9:31

Mark 14:22-24

Matthew 26:26-28

Matthew 26:32

Matthew 26:64

Summary:

Atoning Sacrifice

14. Jesus' atoning blood sacrifice is also taught all throughout the epistles. Look up these passages and summarize what else Scripture teaches about Jesus' sacrifice.

Romans 3:21-26

Romans 5:6-9

Ephesians 1:7; 2:11-19

Colossians 1:19-23

15. After going through all of these scriptures about the atoning work of Christ. It is important to make the distinction that while Jesus' sacrifice was once for all time and all sin, it is not automatically applied to all people. What causes Jesus' sacrifice to be applied to an individual? Use the scriptures that you just looked up in question 14.

16. In Hebrews 10:10-18 it emphasizes Jesus' finished sacrifice that cleanses us from sin and makes us holy or "sanctified." Look through these verses and write down all of the phrases that describe Jesus' sacrifice. By now, you are seeing that the author is repeating himself. Why do you think the author has emphasized these things about Jesus' sacrifice over and over?

17. What does it mean in Hebrews 10:14 when it says that "he has perfected" and how is it related to sanctification? (Use context and word studies of "perfect" and "sanctified" to help you answer.)

A New Covenant Practice

18. Hebrews chapters 8 through 10 make the very important point that when Jesus inaugurated the new covenant, the old covenant, with all its rituals and sacrifices, faded away and became obsolete. (Hebrews 10:9) However, Jesus does leave Christians a religious practice as a part of the new covenant. What are we to do as a symbol of the new covenant? Read Luke 22:19-20.

19. In 1 Corinthians 11:23-29 Paul gives the church more instructions about communion. What do you see in this passage about how we are supposed to celebrate communion. What are the important attitudes and actions?

20. Why do you think Jesus chose this as the way he would like to be remembered?

21. How can you keep this familiar practice fresh? Using what you have learned in this lesson, what meaningful, appropriate worship can you bring to communion?

22. Take some time to add to your "Jesus" list in Lesson 2. What picture of Jesus is developing in your mind?

HOLD ON

Hebrews 10:19-36

The end of Hebrews 10 is a call to action in response to all the teaching up until this point. Our great savior and high priest has been fully described as superior (in his person and his work) to anything previously revealed in the old covenant. Now the writer begins to switch emphasis to descriptions and exhortations of how to live by faith. From here to the end of his letter we will be challenged to hold on to faith, encourage one another, persevere, act, wait, hope, press forward and respond to discipline, all in faith. And this is only the beginning! This week we will see how much we need one another in order to hold on as we live a faithful life.

Summary and Exhortation

1. Read Hebrews 10:19-25. The structure of this passage is a summary of the previous two chapters followed by exhortations. To pull these out, start by listing these key elements:

Summary

Since . . .
(Hebrews 10:19-20)

Since . . .
(Hebrews 10:21)

Exhortations

Let us . . .
(Hebrews 10:22)

Let us . . .
(Hebrews 10:23)

Let us . . .
(Hebrews 10:24)

Let us not . . .
(Hebrews 10:25)

Let us . . .
(Hebrews 10:25)

2. We have covered each of the summary statements from question 1 thoroughly in our previous lessons. Summarize what Hebrews 10:19 -21 means in your own words based on your study over the past weeks.

3. Now let's go back and look at each of these more closely. In Hebrews 10:19 it tells us that our access to the "holy places" is by Jesus' blood sacrifice. In Hebrews 10:20 it describes this as a "new and living way." The Greek word translated as "new" here is only used in this passage in the Bible. Look up this Greek word and connect the definition for "new" to the idea of a living way. What is the irony here?

4. There is an interesting description of what happened when Jesus died in Mark 15:37-38. What is the significance of this dramatic symbolic event? Connect it to Hebrews 10:20.

5. Read Hebrews 10:22 with Hebrews 10:19. Imagine how groundbreaking *assurance* and *confidence* would have been to the Jewish readers of the day. How would these words have affected their view of God and their view of their own access to God?

Draw Near

6. The first exhortation in Hebrews 10:22 is "let us draw near." Think about the assurance of genuine faith in Christ, the clean conscience that Jesus gives and the renewed heart that comes with the new covenant. (Covered in our previous lessons, remember Ezekiel 36:25-27!) How is each of these foundational for you as you draw near to God today? Could you draw near to God without this foundation?

7. To explore more fully what it means to "draw near" or "come," look up the other places this word is used in Hebrews. When a person comes near to Jesus, what can they experience of him?

Hebrews 4:16

Hebrews 7:25

Hebrews 11:6

Hebrews 12:18-24

8. What practical ways do you use to personally draw near to God? What do you talk to him about? What do you offer him? How do you listen to him? Really examine the reality of your nearness to God.

9. When do you draw near? When do you resist drawing near? What could be some factors that play into avoiding nearness to God when we have such amazing access available?

Hold Fast

10. In Hebrews the second exhortation is "let us hold fast the confession of our hope without wavering." One of the ways we hold fast to the confession of our hope is by making sure what we believe is what God has actually revealed of himself. What is the problem if we hold fast to the wrong confession? So, then, what is the confession of our hope?

11. Why was the exhortation to "hold fast the confession of our hope" important for early Jewish believers? Why is it important that the content of the confession be true? Why is it important to hold on no matter what?

12. One of the major themes of the book of Hebrews is perseverance in faith. Look up all these references from Hebrews about holding fast or standing firm in faith and paraphrase each one. How important is it to continue in faith? What does "holding on" reveal about faith?

Hebrews 2:1-3

Hebrews 3:6-14

Hebrews 4:14

Hebrews 6:11-12

Hebrews 10:23

Hebrews 10:35-39

Hebrews 12:1-3

Faithful Promise

13. The end of Hebrews 10:23 gives an assurance. Why does it matter that "he who promised is faithful"?

14. There are many things that can cause doubt and wavering of faith. What have you found shakes your faith? (Some possibilities: intellectual doubts, hard circumstances of life, perceived injustice, etc.) Try to think of a time when your faith wavered. What did you do to combat the doubt?

Good Community

15. In Hebrews 10:24 it gives us the next exhortation: "Let us consider how to stir one another up to love and good works." The Greek word translated as "consider" means "to really think about, to carefully consider." Spend some time thinking about your influence on others. How effective are your words and the example of your life at leading others to greater love and good works? Give an example.

16. The sad truth is that many times our words and life example may stir others up to doubt, anger, gossip, criticism, worldliness, materialism, lust, selfishness or any one of a myriad of things that are the opposite of love and good deeds. Be honest with yourself. Stop and pray about this! What may need to change in your life so that you can be a catalyst for love and good works within the church?

17. Hebrews 10:25 warns us not to develop the habit of neglecting to meet with other Christians and to make a point of encouraging others in light of the return of the savior and the coming judgment. Remember ways that gathering together with other believers for worship and fellowship have caused growth in you. Tell of a time when:

You were in a worship service and God's Spirit spoke to you through the preaching of his Word in that gathering.

You heard a person tell a story of God's faithfulness, and it gave you courage for your situation.

Someone in a Bible study or other small group of believers gave you specific encouragement or prayed for you and it made a difference.

Your church provided you an opportunity to serve that helped you to stretch in faith in a way you would not have done without the help of others.

18. In remembering what you have received by being in Christian community, remember also that this is a mandate for you. Where are you providing this kind of community for others? Describe some ways you are intentionally providing this for others?

19. How does your church connect people to one another to form these kinds of communities? Are you in one of these groups? Why or why not?

20. There is a warning in Hebrews 10:26-31. This way of life is the opposite of the encouraging community we just studied. (We examined a similar passage in Lesson 7.) Summarize this warning.

Remember

21. In Hebrews 10:32-35 the readers are asked to remember something in their past. What circumstances are they asked to remember?

22. What past attitudes of faithfulness are they asked to remember? Why do you think the Hebrew people were able to have these attitudes in their circumstances of suffering?

23. In light of both of these kinds of remembering, what concluding exhortation is in Hebrews 10:35-36? What reward and promise do you see here?

24. One of the ways that we remember God's faithfulness in the midst of trial is to write these things in a journal. Another is to relate the story to others. Take some time to journal here about the growth of your faith through at least one trial or hardship from your life. Consider making regular "remembering" a spiritual discipline!

25. Take time to add anything new from this lesson to your "Jesus" list. By the way, this is another great way to hold fast to your faith in the midst of life. Remember what you know and have experienced of your savior!

FAITH

Hebrews 10:37-11:16

The writer of The Letter to The Hebrews spent the first ten chapters carefully presenting Jesus as superior in every way. He is better than Abraham, Moses and angels. He is the provider of true Sabbath rest, a new type of high priest of the order of Melchizedek, the initiator of the new covenant and the perfect once-for-all blood sacrifice. The writer has encouraged perseverance, warned against faithlessness and reminded of the certainty of judgment. Now he writes with great encouragement and enthusiasm. Having presented Jesus, he now presents the life of faith in Jesus. Knowing all of the trials and doubts the Hebrews face, he cheers them on and provides them with great examples of faith from their own Scriptures.

The Righteous Shall Live by Faith

1. To get a big view of our passage for this lesson read Hebrews 10:35-11:16. Connect the end of Hebrews 10 to Hebrews 11. What is the flow of thought for the writer? Where is he taking the reader?

2. The writer starts by quoting a passage that we see in several other places in Scripture. What does Hebrews 10:38 say and what assurance follows it in 10:39?

3. Now look up these other places in the New Testament that speak about righteousness and faith. What do you find out about the connection between righteousness and faith?

Romans 3:20-26

Galatians 3:10-14

Philippians 3:7-9

Faith Defined

4. Hebrews 11:1 starts with a definition of faith that focuses on how a person experiences it. Look up the Greek words translated as "assurance," "things hoped for," and "conviction." Then, write a paraphrase of Hebrews 11:1.

5. What are the important elements of faith? How is this type of faith different from a wistful hope or wish that something might happen or could be true?

Examples of Faith

6. The writer goes on to use example after example of the kind of faith he has in mind. In other epistles, writers give examples of faithful Christians from other cities living at the same time. Where does the writer to the Hebrews get his examples? Notice where in Scripture he starts and the order of the examples. Why do you think he chose this group of people, and put them in this order?

7. Each of these examples starts with "by faith." The first example is "by faith we." Why do you think he starts with their faith as an example?

8. Why do you think he starts with believing in creation? How does believing in God's creation fit the definition given of faith in Hebrews 11:1?

9. For each of the examples he gives, record what the person did by faith, how he was commended, and the results of faith. (You may have to infer some of these to answer.)

By faith Abel:

By faith Enoch:

By faith Noah:

By faith Abraham:

By faith Abraham and Sarah:
Translators are not sure whether this passage refers to the faith of Sarah or Abraham. (See the difference between NIV and ESV)

10. How do each of these fit the definition of faith in Hebrews 11:1?

God-pleasing Faith

11. In Hebrews 11:6 it tells the reader what it takes to please God. What are two marks of faith? Why do you think both of these are necessary? Could you have one without the other?

12. Let's explore the idea of pleasing God further. Scripture frequently encourages Christians to please God with their lives. Read this sampling of references to support the idea that we please God with our obedience.

Ephesians 5:6-10

Philippians 4:17-18

Colossians 1:9-10

1 Thessalonians 4:1

13. It is a precious truth to Christians that they can please God with their obedience. How could this be a motivation for you to obey as well as an invitation to deeper relationship with God?

14. The idea of pleasing God with our obedience works in tandem with the idea that we are saved by faith alone. How does one go with the other? (Ephesians 2:8-10)

Reward

15. In Hebrews 11:6 it also mentions reward. What kind of reward do you think is spoken of in Hebrews 11:6? (Hebrews 11:5b, 13, 16; 12:22-24; 13:14)

16. We have a tendency to think that when we live a faithful life God owes us the reward we would like, or that our faithfulness somehow should safeguard us from difficulty in this life. What is the danger in this thinking? How might these expectations actually harm our faith?

17. Think of a time in your life when you expected something from God that you didn't get. Talk about the positives and negatives of your reaction. How does your reaction stand up to the definition of faith in Hebrews 11:1 and 11:6?

Strangers on Earth

18. Hebrews 11:13-16 describes a mindset about our time on earth. What attitudes do you see in those who died in faith? What key desire is in Hebrews 11:16?

19. Why are these attitudes and desires key for a faithful life based on the definition from Hebrews 11:1? How can you cultivate these?

20. To understand the idea of being strangers and aliens on the earth read these references. What more do you learn?

Philippians 3:17-21

1 Peter 2:9-11

21. In what ways do you think of yourself as a stranger or exile on this earth? In what ways are you perfectly comfortable here? Think about the tension between the two and write out what you are thinking about this tension here:

Up until this point we have ended our lessons by adding to our list about the attributes of Jesus. Let's start a new list now that compiles what we learn about a faithful follower of Jesus. Turn to the next page and start your list.

TESTED FAITH

Hebrews 11:17-40

By the definition in Hebrews 11:1, faith does not require "sight." At times, obedient faith will fly in the face of tradition (even religious tradition), conventional wisdom, common sense, and even the law of the land. In the second half of Hebrews 11 we see people from the Old Testament defying all of these, choosing instead to act out of faith. Through this faith, these people participated in amazing victories. However, don't forget the rest of the picture! They also endured extreme suffering. In victory or in suffering their faith enabled them to look forward to God's promises even when they did not see them fulfilled. Their example of tested and proven faith stands for eternity.

Tested

1. The first person whose faith we are going to examine is Abraham. Before we do this, we need to look at an important phrase in Hebrews 11:17. The verse starts with, "By faith Abraham, when he was tested." In order to understand our life of faith, we have to understand that God builds faith and reveals the reality of faith through testing. To help understand this, look up these references from the Old Testament and write down what God was testing and how the people did at their test (if applicable).

Exodus 16:4-28

Exodus 20:1-20

Deuteronomy 8:11-16

Judges 3:1-7

2. The Old Testament is literally full of people whose faith and obedience were tested. Many of those tests ended in failure. In fact, even the people mentioned in Hebrews 11 also had tests that they failed. In light of this, why do you think the writer to the Hebrews gives these examples of faith?

3. How does the idea of God testing faith change the way you view the circumstances of life? How could it be a motivator? A warning?

Abraham

4. Let's look at the story of Abraham and Isaac. Read Genesis 22:1-19 along with Hebrews 11:17-19. Observe the story in Genesis and note all of the ways that Abraham demonstrated faith as defined in Hebrews 11:1 and 11:6.

5. Abraham's faith was tested in the extreme, but he did have the benefit of a clear command from God. Are there any clear teachings of Scripture that you find puzzling or difficult to accept? How could Abraham's example help you?

6. Notice the promise to Abraham in Genesis 22:15-18 after he passed the test and God's previous promise in Genesis 13:14-17. What are the main elements of the promises?

Abraham's Line

7. Two important parts of the promise were that the descendants of Abraham would inherit the land and that all nations would be blessed through a descendant of Abraham. What does Hebrews 11:39-40 say about the relationship between the people mentioned in Hebrews 11 and the promise? What ultimate promise is also mentioned here?

8. Many of the faithful mentioned in Hebrews 11 played a role in the fulfillment of the promises to Abraham. Let's start with those mentioned in Hebrews 11 that kept the line of Abraham going to produce a Messiah. Compare the beginning of the genealogy of Jesus in Matthew 1:1-6 to the people mentioned in Hebrews 11:17-32. Who is in both passages?

9. Isaac and Jacob were the son and grandson of Abraham. Both were commended for the fact that they pronounced blessing on the next generation. What about these blessings required faith? What promises to their ancestor Abraham did they look forward to for their sons and grandsons? (Genesis 17:1-8 and Genesis 22:17-18)

10. How did the blessings that Isaac gave also involve deceitfulness? (See Genesis 27.) What might this say about God's sovereignty and about his ability to use all of man's actions for his purposes? Is God limited by our unfaithfulness?

11. Rahab the prostitute is also in the line of Jesus. For what action is she commended in Hebrews 11:31? What do you think would have been the impact for the original readers that a woman was singled out for her faith? A prostitute?

12. What else do you think this says about how God uses people? What do you think this says about how God could use you? What are the important factors in being useful to God?

Joseph

13. Some of the others mentioned in Hebrews 11 acted in faith in regard to entering and defending the Promised Land. Read Hebrews 11:22 along with Genesis 50:24-25 and Exodus 13:19. What promise did Joseph believe? How did he want to be a part of that promise? How did this promise get fulfilled?

14. If you know the story of Joseph, you know that he was sold into slavery by his brothers, but this led him to live a life of great power in Egypt. Why do you think it mattered to him that his bones make it out of Egypt? Despite his worldly success in Egypt, where was his loyalty? Why?

Moses

15. Moses would live out this relationship with the power, influence, and riches of Egypt as well. Read Hebrews 11:23-29. Going phrase-by-phrase, list each action that Moses, his family, or his people took by faith and the motivation behind the actions.

Action   **Motivation**

16. Moses' temptation to pursue status, power, riches, and the pleasures of sin sound very similar to modern temptations. How does your faith and hope for an eternal future also help with these temptations? When have you had to choose to follow God rather than these things?

Triumphs and Tests

17. In Hebrews 11:32 a list of faithful people is included without telling what specifically made them faithful, but there is a list of triumphs of faith in Hebrews 11:33-35a. Compare this list to Hebrews 11:35b-38. What is the contrast?

18. The faithful life includes both amazing triumphs and difficult persecutions. Why is it encouraging to be told both sides of the story?

19. We began this lesson by looking at some Old Testament examples of God's testing. The New Testament also has two major passages that help us process the trials and persecutions that test our faith. Read James 1:2-4, 12-15. What are some important things to know about the origins and purposes of trials and tests?

20. Now read 1 Peter 4:12-16 and Romans 5:1-5. What more do you learn about the origins and purposes of trials? What is the godly way to respond?

21. Compare how you react to trials by the standard found in James, Romans, and 1 Peter. How are you doing by these standards?

22. Re-read Hebrews 11:1-40. It is said that a "test" that is faced with faith becomes an opportunity for a "testimony." What is the testimony of this chapter?

23. What story of faith from your life can you tell as a testimony to the power of faith in Jesus?

24. Take some time to record any new insights you gained from this lesson on what it means to be a follower of Jesus on the list you started in Lesson 14.

RUN THE RACE

Hebrews 12:1-10

After a dramatic presentation of heroes of faith, the author of Hebrews keeps the momentum of encouragement going. He encourages the readers to press forward by leaving behind all the hindrances to a faithful life and by focusing on Jesus who has set the perfect example. He also helps them to get God's perspective on their hardships. God their father is training them up to maturity just as a parent trains a child. God disciplines and trains us as our loving father and leads us to holiness.

A Race

1. In Hebrews 12:1-2 we find a rich passage with emphatic and descriptive language. Get your word study resources ready! To get the big picture you must understand that the faithful life is compared to a race. Look up the Greek word translated as "race" from verse 1. What do you gather about this endeavor? Is this a race for fun, like a playground relay? How do you know?

2. To set the stage for the race analogy, a cloud of witnesses is introduced. A witness in this case is not a watcher, but someone who has knowledge and so can shed light on a subject. Given the context of Hebrews 11, who is this group of witnesses? What knowledge have these witnesses shared?

3. Remember this is a letter that was probably read in one sitting. How does Hebrews 11 set up the exhortations in Hebrews 12? What atmosphere is created?

Weights

4. First, the racer is told to "lay aside every weight." To lay something aside means to put it away, cast it off, or get rid of it. Look up the Greek word translated as "weight." What insight do you get about these weights? What do you think these weights are?

5. Many things can burden us as we seek to live a faithful life. These encumbrances can even be good things that have become distractions. Is there something in your life that hinders faithful living? (Think in terms of activities, work, entertainment, habits, traditions, relationships, etc.)

6. What would it mean to lay these things aside? What would you substitute? Could it be possible to continue in the activity, but to do it with a God-honoring purpose and still be laying it aside? Why, or why not?

Sin

7. In Hebrews 12:1 we are also told to "lay aside the sin which clings so closely." Putting sin aside is a consistent theme in the epistles. Look up these references to get a bigger picture. When we put aside sin, what do we put on? How do we do it?

Ephesians 4:20-32

Colossians 3:5-17

8. What comes to mind for you as you consider putting away sin? What easily entangles you? How do the passages in Ephesians and Colossians give you insight into fighting this specific sin?

Endurance

9. Next this passage tells us to "run with endurance." What does the analogy of an endurance run tell you about the life of faith? (Easy or hard, passive or active, sprint or a marathon, etc.) Read also 1 Corinthians 9:24-27.

10. In your life, what is calling for endurance? Identify at least two areas that you will have to stick with for a long time in order to succeed at living a faithful life.

11. We are told that the race is "set before us." Who sets our race before us? What difference does it make how you think about who is in charge of the course of your life?

Eyes on Jesus

12. In Hebrews 12:2 it tells us our focus should be on Jesus as we run the race of faith. Look up the Greek words translated as "founder" and "perfecter." What do you learn about Jesus?

13. Now read the end of Hebrews 12:2-3. How did Jesus become the founder and perfecter of our faith? What was the joy set before him?

14. What did he have to endure to reach that joy? (Also read Matthew 27:27-31; 45-50.)

15. What from Jesus' example helps us in our race? Why focus on him? How will this help us? (Hebrews 12:3-4)

Discipline

16. In Hebrews 12:5 the analogy changes. Now God is compared to a father who disciplines his child. Look up the Greek word translated as "discipline," which is used nine times in Hebrews 12:5-11. What insight do you gain about this discipline?

17. In Hebrews 12:5-8 the writer reminds them of a passage from Proverbs 3:11-12. What is the critical relationship between discipline and being a son? Can we claim to be a son and forgo discipline?

18. The beginning of the exhortation from Proverbs is "do not regard lightly the discipline of the Lord." There are several ways we can dismiss the discipline of God. Think through these ways of not taking God's training (through difficult circumstances, rebuke, or conviction) seriously. Describe what each would look like:

Hard-hearted, not willing to accept discipline:

Complaining:

Questioning, Arguing:

Defensive, Excuse making:

Denying that a loving God would do this:

19. In our previous lesson we looked at some purposes of suffering and at God's sovereignty in allowing all kinds of character-transforming difficulties and tests. Hebrews 12:5-6 also tells us that some of what we face is chastisement and reproof. What is the difference between suffering persecution and suffering as punishment and correction?

20. Read the example of the Corinthians who were disciplined for misusing communion in 1 Corinthians 11:27-32. What was the discipline from God? What was the purpose of the discipline?

21. While God does chastise, sometimes it is difficult to know if painful circumstances are chastisement. What are some ways you could know if you were being chastised? (Psalm 139:23-24; Hebrews 4:12-13)

22. Another important caution to consider: Should you proclaim that God is chastising someone else? What could be the dangers in this? (Matthew 7:1-6)

Fatherly Discipline

23. Let's go back to Hebrews 12:6-11. The author continues the analogy of a father disciplining a son. How is God's motivation like a father's motivation, only better?

24. How does your relationship with your own earthly father help or hinder your understanding of God's discipline?

25. It is important to understand God's motivation in all kinds of discipline. List all the things you see about God's motivation in discipline and the purpose it serves in the believer's life.

Examine Yourself

26. Take some time to examine yourself. If God's goal in your life is holiness (Hebrews 12:10), what are your goals? How do your goals help or hurt your holiness?

27. Tie Hebrews 12:1-10 together. How does the goal of holiness also relate to Hebrews 12:1-2? What will it take to live a holy life?

28. Take some time to log insights into your list about Jesus and your list about the Faithful Follower in Lesson 14.

SEE TO IT

Hebrews 12:11-17

Chapter 12 of Hebrews is filled with activity. It encourages believers to run the race with endurance by throwing aside hindrances and sin and looking to Jesus' example. It exhorts believers to respond to God's loving, fatherly discipline. Hebrews says this process will not always be pleasant—in fact, often it will be painful! But in the end, because we as believers have a new covenant and a great savior, the process of training will yield "the peaceful fruit of righteousness." It's our job to fully engage in these activities and "see to it" that we don't refuse the God who is speaking.

Training

1. In Hebrews 12:11 the author ties up his teaching on God's discipline, but he also pushes the message forward. What does this verse tell us about discipline's process and what it yields?

2. Let's think a little about this type of training. Look up the Greek word translated as "trained by it" in the ESV. What does this tell you about the training of discipline? When else have you personally experienced that some pain will be involved to produce a good outcome? (Ex. exercise, schooling, music, etc.)

3. Why do you think we resist painful discipline and hard work so strongly in our spiritual lives? What factors in our own nature and our cultural environment play into this? How can we resist these bents?

Fruit

4. We are told this type of discipline and training produces the peaceful fruit of righteousness. Jesus famously taught about fruit production in John 15:1-5. Read this passage and observe it thoroughly. What are the keys to producing fruit according to Jesus? Tie these keys to Hebrews 12.

5. In Hebrews 12:12 it leads us into a group of exhortations. Read Hebrews 12:12-16. For now, just list all the actions from this passage. (Look for the verbs!)

6. It is important to stop at this point and acknowledge that effort is a huge part of Christian growth. It is true that our salvation is by grace through faith and not of ourselves. (Ephesians 2:8-9) Yet once we are saved, we continue to work out our salvation through God's power. (Philippians 2:12-13) Passages like Hebrews 12 affirm that our effort is necessary to grow and to please God. A favorite quote from Dallas Willard: "Grace is opposed to earning, not effort." Ponder this idea and make some notes about how you view spiritual effort.

Keep Going

7. In Hebrews 12:12 the pep talk continues by telling the "runner" from Hebrews 12:1 and the "son" from Hebrews 12:5 to lift drooping hands and strengthen weak knees. Paraphrase this in modern language. Do you use any sayings with the same meaning?

8. The writer may also be alluding to a passage in Isaiah. Read Isaiah 35. What is this passage about? Write down some of the encouraging phrases. If they remembered this passage, how might this allusion have struck the struggling Hebrews?

9. In Hebrews 12:13 the encouragement continues. Read Proverbs 4:20-27. How does someone keep on a straight path spiritually?

10. Those who know Greek syntax emphasize that Hebrews 12:12-13a is addressed in the plural. The idea is that we are to help one another to walk a straight path and strengthen one another when we are fainting or weak. Hebrews 12:13b gives the result of this. What will happen as we look out for the spiritual welfare and obedience of others? Tell a story of when someone has come along side you to help when you were weak.

11. What is the most recent time that you have done this for someone else? Could the example of your life (the path or tracks you leave behind) provide courage for another believer? Why, or why not?

Striving

12. In Hebrews 12:14 it exhorts more action. Look up the Greek word translated as "strive." (ESV) What level of intensity does this indicate?

13. What is the first thing we should strive after in Hebrews 12:14? Read also Matthew 5:9; Romans 12:18 and 1 Peter 3:11. Is there a relationship in your life that lacks peace? What can you do to work hard toward peace?

14. The second thing we are to pursue is holiness. Read also Romans 6:19-22 and 1 Thessalonians 4:1-7. Make any notes on what it means to pursue sanctification. (The same Greek word is translated as both "sanctification" and "holiness.")

15. How does our sanctification relate to eternal life?

16. What have you done in the past to help yourself pursue sanctification or holiness? Think of at least two spiritual disciplines that you could use to strive after holiness.

17. Now think of a specific area of your life where God is working. What is he telling you needs to change in order for you to live a holy life set apart for him? If you are not sure, ask him! (Also read 1 John 2:15-17.)

18. If someone were to come to you with this area that needs to change, to what scriptures would you direct him or her? What plan of action would you recommend? How can you begin to implement this in your own life?

19. Read Galatians 5:16-25. Where do we find the power for change? Connect striving for holiness with the source of power. How do they complement one another?

Bitterness

20. Remember the context of Hebrews. Many hearers of the letter are not yet fully committed to Christ and are tempted to go back to Judaism. Therefore, the next section is a warning again about failing to enter into the life of true faith. Hebrews 12:15 alludes to Deuteronomy 29:16-29. Read this passage to understand the meaning of this root of bitterness. How would this kind of rebellion cause someone to miss the grace of God?

21. While idolatry and unbelief produce bitter fruit, small grievances can also turn into bitterness. Are there any ways that bitterness may be leading to unbelief, unfaithfulness or thanklessness in your life? How will you prevent this bitterness from growing and poisoning your relationship with God and others?

Esau's Error

22. In Hebrews 12:16-17 Esau is a foolish example. Read Genesis 25:29-34. For what did Esau trade his birthright? Why? Tie this to the sexually immoral and unholy behavior warned against in Hebrews 12:16. What do these temptations have in common?

23. In Genesis 27 it tells the story of how Jacob tricked Isaac into giving him a blessing ahead of Esau. While this was unfair, Esau's reaction to it tells something about him. Read Genesis 27:34-41. Notice how Esau describes the loss of his birthright and how he reacts to Jacob's blessing. What about Esau's life is a negative example?

24. What is a godly way to react when life doesn't turn out the way you think it should? Use Scripture to back up your answer.

25. Review this lesson. Distill what you have learned about your life as a faithful follower of Jesus and add it to your list in Lesson 14.

COME TO THE MOUNTAIN

Hebrews 12:18-29

Chapter 12 of Hebrews ends with a rousing call to remember God's power and the greatness of the new covenant kingdom he established in Christ. The old covenant is represented by the fear at Mount Sinai and is based on law. Mount Zion represents the new covenant and its blessings that come to believers in salvation. In light of this great new covenant kingdom, the final words of Hebrews 12 remind us to listen to God who speaks, to approach him with thankfulness and to worship with reverence and awe!

Leave Behind

1. Most of Hebrews 12 up to this point has been a strong exhortation to run the race of life in faithfulness, accepting God's discipline with an eye toward maturity and fruitfulness. In Hebrews 12:18-24 the readers are reminded how the Christian life is different from the life they leave behind in Judaism. Hebrews 12:18 begins the section with, "For you have not come." To understand what he is summarizing, read Exodus 19:10-20:19. For each phrase of Hebrews 12 below, write in the corresponding verses from Exodus.

Come to what may be touched

A blazing fire

Darkness

Gloom

A tempest

The sound of a trumpet

A voice

Whose words made the hearers beg no more be spoken

For they could not endure the order . . . if even a beast touches the mountain, it shall be stoned

2. The Ten Commandments were given at this time. Why do you think God created the atmosphere that he did at this event? What did the atmosphere say about his character and about the position of the people in relationship to God? What did it say about the seriousness of the law?

The New

3. In Hebrews 12:22-24 it presents a stark contrast to Hebrews 12:18-21. To understand, we have to start with the concept of Zion. The mountain of the new covenant is Mount Zion, representing the heavenly Jerusalem. Sinai symbolizes law, but Zion symbolizes grace. The writer to the Hebrews reminds his wavering readers that they are not coming to Sinai but to Zion. According to Hebrews 12:22-24, who is in the heavenly Jerusalem? List them all.

4. How is it that the readers "have come" to this place already? (2 Corinthians 5:16-18; Colossians 1:12-14)

5. From these descriptions what sets Zion apart from Sinai? What makes the new covenant better than the old?

6. Re-read Hebrews 12:18-24. What encouragement is here for the new Jewish Christian? Why include this right after talking about discipline and running the race of faith?

7. In 2 Corinthians 3:4-11 Paul supports the ideas of Hebrews 12. What does 2 Corinthians 3:4-11 say about the relative value of the ministry of the law and the ministry of the Spirit? What is better about the ministry of the Spirit?

8. In 2 Corinthians 3:12-16 it describes the contrast between the way of the law and the new way in the Spirit. Observe this passage carefully and list all the contrasts you see.

9. In 2 Corinthians 3:17-18 Paul tells us what the benefits of life in the Spirit are. List them, and paraphrase what they mean.

10. How have you seen this transformation at work in your life or in the life of someone you know? Give an example.

11. In Hebrews 12:25 it transitions with another warning. Remember all of Hebrews 12 including the verses about the Lord's discipline. Expand this warning to include all that has been said so far in Hebrews 12. Why shouldn't we refuse God? Think of at least two positive reasons along with the negative reasons.

12. In Hebrews 12:26 it reminds us of the voice that shook the earth at Sinai. It also ties it to a future time when "shaking" will come again. What is this shaking, and what is its purpose? (Hebrews 12:26-27; Haggai 2:6-9; 2 Peter 3:10-12 and Revelation 21:1-2)

Thankful Worship

13. In Hebrews 12:28 the author tells us to be thankful for our unshakable kingdom. Let's review by surveying what the book of Hebrews has said so far about the unshakeable kingdom that we receive through salvation. For each reference what could make you thankful for salvation?

Hebrews

1:3

1:8

2:10-11

2:14

2:15

2:18

4:14-16

6:17-20

7:26-27

8:10

9:11-12

9:13-14

9:15

9:26-28

10:10

10:39

11:39-40

12:22-24

14. What does it do for your faith to remember the blessings and surety of salvation? What can you do to remember your salvation as a habit? How is this also fuel for worship?

15. In Hebrews 12:28 it also tells us to offer acceptable worship with reverence and awe. From these verses, what are the elements of worship?

1 Chronicles 16:23-34

Psalm 95:1-6

Psalm 96:1-9

John 4:19-24

Romans 12:1

Hebrews 12:28-29

16. Based on these scriptures write a definition of worship.

17. What worship methods best lead you to worship with reverence and awe? Think about both corporate worship and your private worship.

18. Is there anything in your worship that may lead you to take God too lightly? Is there anything that causes you to focus on your tastes or your experience rather than God? How can you change these things or your attitude about these things so that you are giving God the worship that he desires?

19. Take some time here to go back to your "Faithful Follower" list in lesson 14 and add to it.

20. Look back at your "Jesus" list, and spend some time writing out praise and worship with reverence and awe.

LIVE IT

Hebrews 13:1-6

We are nearing the end of our study of the book of Hebrews. We have pondered the ways that Jesus is superior to all that God had revealed through Judaism up until his coming. We have looked deeply into Jesus as the great high priest. We have examined his atoning blood sacrifice. We have heard the warnings about perseverance in the faith. We have heard encouragement to live a life of faith with endurance. Now, at the end of the letter, we are given a series of practical instructions for how to live because of these great doctrines. Right belief must produce right behavior! Get ready: this is where it all becomes even more practical!

Brotherly Love

1. The first exhortation in Hebrews 13 is "let brotherly love continue." Start by looking up the Greek word translated as "brotherly love." What are the characteristics of this love?

2. When you cross-reference the Greek word *philadelphia*, you find these passages that describe what it means to live in brotherly love. Where does this love come from? How is it lived out?

Romans 12:9-13

1 Thessalonians 4:9-10

1 Peter 1:22-23

2 Peter 1:3-8

3. Brotherly love is important for many reasons. Look up these verses to see what love for other Christians shows and to whom.

John 13:35

1 John 3:14-19

4. What do you think non-Christians think of you? Would "love" be one of the first descriptions they use for you? Why or why not?

One Another

5. Throughout the New Testament we are given many instructions on how to treat "one another" as Christians. Read through the list of "one another" verses on the next page. Tell a story of a time you have seen one or more of these lived out well by another believer.

One Another

- Be devoted to one another in brotherly love. (Romans 12:10)
- Honor one another above yourselves. (Romans 12:10)
- Live in harmony with one another. (Romans 12:10)
- Stop passing judgment on one another. (Romans 14:13)
- Instruct one another. (Romans 15:14)
- Accept one another, as Christ accepted you. (Romans 15:7)
- Greet one another with a holy kiss. (Romans 16:16)
- When you come together to eat, wait for each other. (1 Corinthians 11:33)
- Have equal concern for each other. (1 Corinthians 12:25)
- Serve one another in love. (Galatians 5:15)
- Carry each other's burdens. (Galatians 6:2)
- Be patient, bearing with one another in love. (Ephesians 4:2)
- Be kind and compassionate to one another. (Ephesians 4:32)
- Forgiving each other as God in Christ has forgiven you… (Ephesians 4:32)
- Speak to one another with psalms, hymns, and spiritual songs. (Ephesians 5:19)
- Submit to one another out of reverence for Christ. (Ephesians 5:21)
- In humility, consider others better than yourselves. (Philippians 2:3)
- Do not lie to each other. (Colossians 3:9)
- Bear with each other. (Colossians 3:13)
- Admonish one another. (Colossians 3:16)
- Make your love increase and overflow for each other. (1 Thessalonians 3:12)
- Encourage one another. (1 Thessalonians 4:18)
- Build each other up. (1 Thessalonians 5:11)
- Spur one another on to love and good deeds. (Hebrews 10:24)
- Do not slander one another. (James 4:11)
- Don't grumble against each other. (James 5:9)
- Offer hospitality to one another. (1 Peter 4:9)
- Wash one another's feet. (John 13:14)

6. Is there anything on this list that jumped out to you as something that you have neglected as a part of your brotherly love? What can you do to live more fully in that part of Christian love?

Hospitality

7. Hospitality was important in the ancient world. There were few inns and they were often dangerous. Hospitality included the idea of caring for the needs of others, not just parties or friendly gatherings. Read Hebrews 13:2 and these scriptures where hospitality is mentioned. What do you learn about who should practice hospitality, to whom, and how.

Romans 12:13

1 Timothy 3:2

1 Timothy 5:9-10

Titus 1:7-8

Hebrews 13:2

1 Peter 4:9

8. Describe someone you know whom you think practices hospitality beautifully. What are some of the marks of true hospitality? How is hospitality different from "entertaining"? (mood, focus, duration, need etc.)

9. What can you do to grow in hospitality? What keeps you from practicing this vital part of the Christian life? Think this through and make an actual plan!

10. In Hebrews 13:3 it tells the reader to remember those in prison. Why might this have special significance for the Hebrews? (Hebrews 10:34) What attitude are they to have toward those in prison? Why?

11. Jesus taught specifically about hospitality to strangers and prisoners in Matthew 25:31-46. This teaching came on the Tuesday before Jesus was crucified. Observe this passage carefully using the "who, what, where, when, why, how" questions. What is Jesus saying? Why was he leaving this as one of his last teachings?

12. Focus specifically on those in prison. Think especially of those who are in prison because of their faith. According to Hebrews 13:3, what obligation do we have as Christians? Why? What are some ways to live this out?

Marriage

13. In Hebrews 13:4 it brings up the topic of marriage and sex. The first exhortation is "let marriage be held in honor among all." Look up the Greek word translated as "held in honor." (ESV) What are some ways you could treat marriage in this way?

14. Let's look at Ephesians 5:22-33 to see what an honorable marriage looks like. Go through this passage and record what it says a wife and husband will be like if behaving honorably.

Wife

Husband

15. How does a good marriage provide a picture of Christ and the church? How does this add to the preciousness of marriage?

16. In light of all the ways marriage is failing in our society (living together without marriage, divorce, abuse, same-sex marriage, adultery, etc.) how might a healthy marriage be counter-cultural and a profound witness? Have you experienced this?

17. What happens to our witness to the unbelieving world when we don't treat marriage differently than our culture does? How can this be redeemed? If you are married, what can you do to move toward a marriage that is a picture of Christ and the church? Think of something specific.

Sex

18. The second half of Hebrews 13:4 addresses sexual behavior. What does this verse specifically warn against?

19. Scripture has a lot to say about sex. Look up these passages and write down specifically how the marriage bed can be defiled.

Matthew 5:27-30

Matthew 5:31-32

1 Corinthians 6:9-11

Ephesians 5:5

20. In Song of Songs 5:2-6 it describes a scenario that may also cause trouble in the marriage bed. What is going on here, and how might this cause sin in marriage? Read also 1 Corinthians 7:1-5 for more insight.

21. As Christians we have a tendency to want to judge and censure those who are not believers based on their sinful sexual behavior. What does 1 Corinthians 5:9-13 say about this? Who are we supposed to hold accountable?

22. Look at your own life now. Whether you are single or married you must live out your sexuality in a God-honoring, marriage-honoring way. How specifically can *you* do this? What might you need to stop doing? Start doing?

Be Content

23. Let's finish up this lesson with Hebrews 13:5. Also read 1 Timothy 6:6-10 and Philippians 4:11-13. Observe these passages very carefully. What does it mean to be content? What is the benefit of contentment?

24. Continuing in 1 Timothy 6:6-10, what is the danger of desiring to be rich and loving money?

25. What does Hebrews 13:5-6 give as a reason for contentment? Talk about how fear and lack of faith play into our insecurity and lack of contentment financially.

26. Tie this whole lesson together. Why does it matter how we live our lives? What does it show?

27. Spend some time logging in what you have learned on your "Faithful Follower" list in lesson 14.

LEADERS AND FOLLOWERS

Hebrews 13:7-25

We finish the book of Hebrews by continuing to look at what it means to live the life of a faithful follower of Jesus. One of the important parts of the Christian life is learning how to follow the people who lead and teach, and how to discern which of their teachings to follow. Therefore, in this last lesson, we are going to take a look at what it takes to be a godly leader worth following and what it takes to be a godly follower who is a joy to lead!

Godly Leaders

1. In Hebrews 13:7 it introduces leadership as a new source of strength for the Christian life. Leaders are identified here as those who spoke the word of God to them. In 2 Timothy 3:14-4:2 Paul gave Timothy instructions regarding the teaching of the word. What is the job of Scripture? (2 Timothy 3:14-17)

2. What then are leaders to do with Scripture? (2 Timothy 4:1-2)

3. What is one of the key qualifications for a leader worth following, therefore? How should you relate to a leader who does not meet this qualification?

4. What three things should the Hebrews do regarding leaders according to Hebrews 13:7?

5. Other scriptures give qualifications for leadership that describe a godly lifestyle. Look up these references and make a list of the types of behavior that are worth considering and imitating.

1 Timothy 3:1-13

2 Timothy 2:15-16, 22-25

Titus 1:5-9

Titus 2:1-3

6. At least one of the reasons for these qualifications is so that leaders will be godly examples to follow. Which means, of course, these are standards that any believer should be moving toward. Evaluate yourself by the list of qualifications from question 5. Can you echo what Paul says in Philippians 3:17? Why or why not?

Led Away to Strange Teaching

7. In Hebrews 13:8 it reminds us that Jesus is the same yesterday, today, and forever. The application of this comes in Hebrews 13:9. If Jesus is the same, then doctrine about a Christ-honoring life is also timeless. What is the instruction in Hebrews 13:9?

8. The practical issue at hand is what to do with ceremonial foods. What does the New Testament teach about food according to these verses?

Acts 10:14-16

Romans 14:17-21

9. Similar instructions about other "strange and diverse" teachings are all over the epistles. Look up these cross-references and note *what* teachings are to be avoided and *why*.

Galatians 1:6-9

Galatians 5:1-6

Colossians 2:8

Colossians 2:16-23

Titus 1:10-16

10. What do you do when you hear teaching that you think may be questionable? How do you evaluate a leader's teaching? What standards do you use? (Acts 17:11)

Jesus' Altar

11. In Hebrews 13:10-13 it contrasts the sacrifices that priests made at altars with the sacrifice Jesus made. In order to understand this passage, we need to go back to Leviticus. Read Leviticus 4:16-21. Make note of what was sacrificed, where it was sacrificed and why it was sacrificed.

12. Now read Hebrews 13:10. If the priests who served in the tent made this kind of sacrifice for sin at their altar, on what "altar" was Jesus' sacrifice made? Why can't those who hold to Jewish sacrifices "eat" (metaphorically) from this altar?

13. In Hebrews 13:11-12, to what is Jesus compared and how is he similar?

14. What are the Hebrews told to do in light of this according to Hebrews 13:13? How could going to Jesus bring reproach on them?

15. Why can they endure reproach according to Hebrews 13:14? Have you ever had to bear reproach for your faith in Jesus? Tell the story here. How does the encouragement to the Hebrews in this verse also encourage you?

Our Sacrifices

16. If Jesus is our sacrifice for sin, we no longer have to make a sacrifice for sin. However, in Hebrews 13:15-16 it tells us there are sacrifices we make. What are they? Remembering all we've been learning, why do you think the author links these two sacrifices? How important is it for a believer to do both?

17. What does Hebrews 13:17 instruct the reader to do? What reason does the verse give for doing this?

Leadership

18. Beyond being an example to others by their godly lifestyle, Jesus gave leaders a standard by which they must lead. Read Matthew 20:25-28 and John 13:12-17. What is the standard of leadership?

19. The Greek word translated as "keeping watch" literally means "losing sleep over." If your pastor is losing sleep over your soul and bearing extra accountability, what can you do to be a joy? Think of something specific!

20. How could a follower's behavior be a source of "groaning" for leaders? Think of some specific behaviors or examples.

21. When a leader makes a decision that is doctrinally sound but may go against one of your traditions or preferences, why is it crucial to handle submission and obedience well? What is at stake?

22. How can you make sure that you respond well? How can you help others to respond in a godly way? What should you do? What shouldn't you do?

23. Is there a command or instruction by a leader to which you should not submit nor obey? What factors play into this? How do you recognize abuse of authority?

Prayer

24. In Hebrews 13:18-21 the writer asks for prayer and offers a benedictory prayer for his readers. Paraphrase the content of each of these prayers.

25. How do these prayers help summarize the message of the letter?

26. Take some time to pray these prayers for the leaders and followers of your church. Consider committing a time to pray regularly for the leaders and followers of your church.

27. Read Hebrews 13:22. Take time to log all you have learned in this lesson about being a faithful follower of Jesus on your list in Lesson 14.

28. Now take some time to review your list in Lesson 14. What have you learned this year that you want to remember? What would help you "bear with my word of exhortation" as it says in Hebrews 13:22?

LIFE STORY DAYS

Life Story Days

I first learned about using life stories to build true fellowship within a group from Susie Sartarelli. She called these days of life sharing "Tapestry." The Tapestry Story questions were designed to create an opportunity for each participant to tell their own story. Our Life Story Days follow in the footsteps of these "Tapestry" group sessions.

Each Life Story Day will be guided by a question that prompts the storytelling for that day. You'll find these questions, with a blank page for you to write out your thoughts, on the pages that follow. You will prepare about a 10-minute story, based on the prompt, that shares your own unique life experience. With this presentation each person will have the opportunity to open up his or her life to the members of the group. Photos are often helpful in telling your story and writing your story will help you be clear and focused as you present. Use your own discretion to decide the level of personal detail that you share but make it your aim to be truthful and open without needlessly exposing the other people in your stories.

The purpose of Life Story Day is to encourage authentic fellowship. As we share our stories we have the opportunity to understand one another more fully and love one another deeply. We can take off the masks and show our true selves. No need to present only the best version of yourself! You are free to be honest.

The sharing in Life Story Day can be a powerful experience. It is important to remember that the purpose of Life Story Day is to deepen relationship, not to solve each other's problems. It is critical to listen without judging to each member of your group and then to let the story stand as a gift to the group. The storyteller's life is not open for discussion at this time. Often, a member will share something that they have previously been afraid or ashamed to share with others. We receive this kind of sharing with compassion and thankfulness for the courage and trust it requires.

It is absolutely critical that each story is kept in complete confidence (see the Brooklyn Dodger's Clubhouse Rule.) Under no circumstances are these stories to be shared without permission outside the group, even with the names removed. This level of confidentiality is hard, but it is crucial for each member to feel safe within the group. This is how bonds of love, fellowship, trust and loyalty are forged.

Life Story 1
My Family

Tell us a story about your family of origin that illustrates how your family has shaped you as a person.

Life Story 2
My Spiritual Journey

Tell the story of how you came to believe in Jesus as your savior. How did you become aware of your own sin? Who told you about Jesus? What circumstances led you to believe? How has your life changed since coming to faith?

Life Story 3
A Great Joy

Tell a story of a great joy in your life. How has this joy affected the way you view God, self and others?

Life Story 4
Life-Giving Reproof

Tell a story of when you had a friend or family member give you life-changing reproof. What was the situation and how did you respond? What happened to the relationship with this friend or family member? How do you think God was involved in this confrontation?

The Brooklyn Dodgers Clubhouse Rule:

What you see in here and hear in here,
stays in here when you leave here.

Doubtless, when the baseball team made this rule it was to hide some of the mischief that went on in the clubhouse! Nevertheless, the rule created a bond between brothers. For us, the rule is not so that we can hide but to provide an environment where we can stop hiding. Christians often feel like they are alone in experiencing the pains and struggles of life. When they look around at church, others seem to have it all together. Don't believe it! Even the most outwardly perfect life is touched with pain of one kind or another. When we create safe places to tell the truth about our lives power is released from within the body of Christ to support, comfort and love one another. No one is alone in pain or the struggle toward godly living!

Confidentiality is the key to loyalty and deep fellowship within a group. When participants know they will not be subjected to gossip, they feel safe to reveal themselves. Gossip is a sin and a destroyer of fellowship within the body of Christ and especially within a small group. We must never talk negatively about another behind his or her back. This is a high call, and hard to achieve. **Within our groups nothing that is shared within the group should be shared outside the group without permission.** Period. Even to spouses. Even with names removed.

Unfortunately, sometimes this trust is broken within a group. Someone tells a story without permission. In that case, confession of the broken trust, to the group, is called for. Forgiveness and grace can then be extended, and fellowship restored. We learn to forgive others as we have been forgiven, and even in this, fellowship can be deepened.

STUDY AIDS

Observation

A great skill to begin your Bible study is observation. Observation is the process of asking questions of the passage to determine what it says. You are looking for the obvious and the objective. Think: "What does the passage actually say?" not "What do I think or feel about it?" and not "How should I respond to it?" After all, don't we need to understand what a passage is saying before we decide what to think and do about it?

Many observation questions are built into this study. You will find charts to complete and lists to make. Occasionally, in this study you will be asked to "observe" a verse or passage of scripture. The word "observe" is a cue to look at the text objectively. There are many ways to make observations of a passage. Most of them involve reading with a purpose in mind. Here are some prompts that will help you make objective observations:

- Ask who, what, when, where, why and how of the passage. (Ex. What do I find out about God from this passage? What do I find out about the main character of this story? Who is mentioned in this passage? When did this take place? Etc.)

- Notice what the author says about himself, his audience and God

- Notice time and place

- Make lists of what you observe.

- Look for words that are repeated.

- Look for words that are unfamiliar.

- Look for contrasts.

- Look for comparisons.

- Look for transition words such as: but, and, therefore, since etc. Then look back to see the context and connections these words are pointing to.

- Look for concepts that are emphasized.

- Make a note of anything you don't understand or would like to know more about.

Cross-References

Cross-referencing is a useful skill to interpret (discern the meaning of) a text. To cross-reference means to find other places in Scripture that:

- Contain the same words
- Contain similar phrases
- Provide more teaching on the same concepts or topics
- Contain direct quotes from other places in Scripture

1. Cross-reference or find other places where a certain word is used.
   - Use the concordance in your study Bible or one such as *Strong's Complete Concordance* to search for the same <u>English</u> words.
   - Use a concordance to find the same Greek or Hebrew words.

2. This leads to a topical study. Both kinds of word studies will help you discover what Scripture says on a given topic.
   - Often searching for opposite words will also help flesh out the meaning of a topic.
   - Searching synonyms will also lead to more teaching on a topic.

3. Cross-reference to find similar phrases.
   - These cross-references are found in the margin of a study Bible. The phrase is marked with a lowercase letter above that phrase in the text and that letter corresponds to a list of references in the margin.
   - These will depend on the scholar who has compiled the cross-references, so it is often wise to consult several study Bibles.
   - Also check the cross-references from the verses that were cross-referenced from your original verse. Following this trail often adds more information to your original search.

4. Cross-reference direct quotes.
   - These are also found in the margin of a study Bible.
   - Look these up to read the quote from its original context.
   - There are many, many Old Testament references in the New Testament. The original context will help you understand the new usage.
   - Jesus often quoted the Old Testament.

Word Study

The Bible is an ancient book originally written in ancient languages: Hebrew, Aramaic, and Greek. The first translations of the Bible were from these original languages into Latin. Throughout history a series of translations have been made into other commonly spoken languages such as English.

Modern translations (such as the NASB, ESV, and NIV) translate from the earliest documents of the original languages into the English words we use today. Language is fluid, so when you read your modern translation, you are reading the work of many men making their best linguistic effort to convey what the text said in the original. Very little is "lost in translation," so you can be confident in the Bible you have in your hands.

That being said, often we understand less than we think we do, and are unsure of the meaning even of English words. In addition, there are often nuances in the original languages that don't get captured completely by English. You can discover much by doing a basic word study.

What words should you look up?

- Any word that you don't understand
- Any word that seems critical to the meaning of the passage
- Repeated key words
- Words that you wouldn't use in normal conversation that seem especially unique to the Bible (like "grace" or "blessed")
- Places or people that are not familiar

Word Study Step by Step

Step1:
Look up your word in the alphabetical listing of an exhaustive concordance.
Use an exhaustive concordance keyed to the translation you are using. *Strong's Exhaustive Concordance* is keyed to the King James Version, but you can access others keyed to the version of the Bible you are using. These are available in book form or for free online. Blue Letter Bible is a popular online concordance/study tool: www.blueletterbible.org. If you use the online versions, you will use their search engines and procedures rather than this "step-by-step" which is designed for traditional references. Blue Letter Bible has tutorials on the site or you can view a tutorial I made here: https://envolvemedia.adobeconnect.com/_a984979381/blbtutorial

Step2:
Scan the list of references to find the verse that contained the word you are studying.
There are often several Hebrew or Greek words that are translated into one English word, so it is important to locate your reference.

Step 3:
Make a note of the number that the concordance has assigned to that particular word.

Step 4:
Using that number, go to the numerical listing in the "dictionary" section in the back of the concordance and find the Greek or Hebrew word that corresponds to the number.

Step 5:
Write the Greek or Hebrew word and make notes on the definition found in that "dictionary."

Step 6:
Look up the English word numerically or alphabetically in an expository Bible dictionary.
Vine's Expository Dictionary is a good basic resource. Make sure you are looking at the definition for the Greek (or Hebrew) keyed word from your passage. Make notes of what the dictionary says for that Greek or Hebrew word in your particular passage. Spiros Zodhiates' *Complete Word Study Dictionary* is also a great resource for the New Testament. Its entries are listed by the Strong's concordance number. For Hebrew, *The Complete Word Study Dictionary: Old Testament* is a good resource. (You can find details for both in the bibliography.)

Step 7:
Now look up the word in an English dictionary.
Often there are multiple definitions for a single English word. You must use context to determine which definition is applicable to your passage.

Step 8:
Use all the information you have gathered to define the word you are studying.
Often it is helpful to use all your gathered information to paraphrase the definition. This will stretch you, but it will help clarify the meaning for you.

Other helpful uses of the Exhaustive Concordance:

1. Note all the other places that particular Greek (or Hebrew) word is used. (Is it a common or uncommon word?)

2. Look up some of the other places that word is used. Often those references, in context, will also give you insight into the usage in your passage. Using blueletterbible.org makes this easy.

3. These references will also help you cross-reference the full counsel of scripture on that topic. You can make a list of your findings on a particular topic.

4. Make special note of the places where the author of your particular book has used that word. Usage is often very consistent within an author's writing.

5. Note what other Greek (or Hebrew) words are translated into the same English word. See if you can make distinctions between these passages and meanings.

Made in United States
Orlando, FL
03 December 2024

54919798R00143